Blame Not the Wind

Blame Not the Wind

A tragedy at sea
A cover-up
One mother's search for justice

Shirley Cooklin

HarperElement
An imprint of HarperCollins*Publishers*
1 London Bridge Street
London SE1 9GF

www.harpercollins.co.uk

HarperCollins*Publishers*
Macken House, 39/40 Mayor Street Upper
Dublin 1, D01 C9W8, Ireland

First published by HarperElement 2025

1 3 5 7 9 10 8 6 4 2

A catalogue record of this book is available from the British Library

ISBN 978-0-00-876766-2

Printed and bound in the UK using 100% renewable
electricity at CPI Group (UK) Ltd

For Tine – who brought the gift of love to Ben's short life

THE CAST

THE FAMILY

Ben Bryant: an 18-year-old sailor
Shirley Cooklin: his mother
Becca Bryant: her 20-year-old daughter
Peter Bryant: her ex-husband & father to both children
Alan Cooklin: Shirley's brother, a doctor
Fiz: his wife
Charley, Danny, Lisa: their children & Ben's cousins

FRIENDS OF THE FAMILY

Lew and Rosalie
Beryl Bainbridge: a novelist
Joan Bakewell: a broadcaster
Jan: a theatre producer
David: a BBC Radio producer
Sally Lahee: an actor
John Goldsmith: a writer
Anthea: his wife
Tine Joustra: Ben's Dutch girlfriend
Mrs Joustra: her mother
David Goldberg: a Rabbi
Jack: a stallholder at Queen's Crescent Market

THE CAST

AT HEATHROW AIRPORT
Rosina and John Messer-Bennetts: bereaved parents
John Hamilton: a previous Captain
Elizabeth: his wife
Mungo: a ship's cook from the *Inca*
Colin Seale: Race Director for the STA
Bobby Cooper: Ben's best friend, a survivor
Ron Cooper: Bobby's father
Andy Freeman: a survivor & ship's engineer

MARQUES SAILORS (past and present)
Charlie Lanyon: a previous First Mate
Denis Orde: survivor & First Mate at the time of the disaster
Iain Cuthbertson: an actor who previously filmed on *Marques*

JOINT OWNERS OF *MARQUES*
Mark Litchfield & Robin Cecil-Wright*

THE GOVERNMENT
Rt Hon. Margaret Thatcher: Prime Minister
Nicholas Ridley: her Minister for Transport
Frank Dobson: Shirley's Member of Parliament

---

* Note that the ownership was disputed.

THE CAST

IN THE USA

Karen Davidson: an attorney in Maine
Doug Skinner: an attorney
Bill Peterson: Commander in US Navy/expert on old sailing craft & brother to Susan Howell (ASTA official who drowned)
Roger Long: expert working with Bill Peterson

AT THE *SUNDAY TIMES*

David Sinclair: Deputy Editor
Peter Robinson: Managing Editor
Mick Brown: a reporter

VARIOUS

Simon: a local 'beat' police officer
Nicola Shearer: a *BBC Newsnight* producer
Jenni Murray: *Woman's Hour* presenter
Louis Blom-Cooper: a QC & friend of Shirley
The Lord Napier & Ettrick: peer of the realm & PPS to HRH Princess Margaret
John Perryman: Mark Litchfield's private advisor
Terry Eastwood: CPS or Crown Prosecution Service
Alex: a plain-clothes officer, Devon & Cornwall CID

LAWYERS TAKING PART IN THE PUBLIC INQUIRY

Rufus Stone QC: aka Commissioner to the Public Inquiry
John Reeder QC: for Nicholas Ridley, Minister for Transport

THE CAST

Peter Gross: his number two
Jervis Kay: for STA & ASTA (US & UK Sail Training Associations)
Mr Perry: for Mark Litchfield
Belinda Bucknall: for Lloyd's the Insurers
Rupert Massey: for Shirley
Dwayne D. Fitzgerald: US attorney working with Bill Peterson

SURVEYORS AT DEPARTMENT FOR TRANSPORT
Darlow, Longbottom, Noble and Holstead
John Perryman

S. V. *MARQUES*

CURRICULUM VITAE

1917   Built at Valencia, Spain. Traded under sail as 2-M Schooner 'pailebot', mainly in Mediterranean.

1928   Single main engine installed. Trading continued, now as 'moto-velero'.

1930s   Believed suffered bomb damage during Civil War while hauled out of the water.

1940s   Rebuilt. Traded again, mostly with cargoes of beer from Tarragona to Mallorca.

1960s   Main engine replaced by twin Kelvin layout, working out of Palma, Mallorca. Use of sails largely discontinued.

1970   Trading operations ceased. Lay in Palma.

1972   Bought by Robin Cecil-Wright and brought to England.

1972–74   Re-rigged and re-fitted as 2-M Brigantine, by owner's men, in Southampton. Hold converted for accommodation.

1975–76 Based between Falmouth and Charlestown, Cornwall. Activities included:
Trip to South Brittany
The Fight Against Slavery (BBC TV) at Dartmouth
Songs of Praise (BBC TV) at Charlestown
Poldark (BBC TV)
Voyage to Bordeaux for consignment of wine (*Sunday Times* Wine Club)
Diving charter to Brittany
The Onedin Line (BBC TV)
At Dartmouth and Exeter (masts had to be lowered and sent up again).

1976–77 Re-rigged and re-fitted at Charlestown as 3-M Barque, by owner's men, to represent HMS *Beagle*. Mark Litchfield became half-owner.

1977–78 20,000-mile voyage as HMS *Beagle* in *The Voyage of Charles Darwin* (BBC TV) round South America via Magellan Straits, the Galapagos Islands and Panama.

1978 Tall Ships Race to Oslo and back with 18 trainees. *Kidnapped* (TV).
Dracula (Universal Pictures) with Laurence Olivier on board.

1979 Five-month refit at Charlestown and Fowey.
Robinson Crusoe (Belgian TV) in Holland.
Trials for Jubilee Sailing Trust reconstruction of sailing ship for the disabled.

The Commanding Sea (TV) at Portsmouth. Promotional photography for Horrockses Fashion and for German 'Code Wind' cigarettes. Cruise for Richard Demarco Gallery with artists, poets and writers to Wales, Ireland, Scillies and Brittany.

1980   Seven months in Canary Islands operating two-week cruises among islands for parties flown from England.

Two months' round-Britain voyage for Richard Demarco Gallery with parties of artists, poets and writers, calling at over 20 ports.

1981   Refit at Barbate de Franco, SW Spain. Masts extended to include 'royals' and 'stunsails' added.

Sonata de Estio (Spanish TV) at Barbate.

Four months in western Mediterranean running 10- to 14-day cruises for parties brought from England in ship's double-decker bus.

Included some very severe weather.

1982   Continuation of refit. A number of planks replaced etc. and new keel fitted.

Returned to England with token cargo of Domecq sherry for Bristol Wine Fair.

Die Eisenbahn (German TV) in Bristol Channel and Gloucester.

'Clipper Challenge' round-Britain race with *Ciudad de Inca* for the British Electric Traction Co. plc. In two and a half months the ships gave experience of square-rigged sailing in all weathers to some 220 teenagers of all backgrounds. Thirty ports were visited, 41 receptions held at which 2,500 guests were entertained on board, over 115 articles with photographs appeared in national and local press, over 30 radio interviews were broadcast, and 32 television crews filmed the ships.

The Eternal Sea (Disney, for Disneyland, Tokyo) at Charlestown.

Jamaica Inn (HTV) off Padstow, north Cornwall.

1983   Summer voyage to Scillies, Lisbon and Azores.

Master of Ballantrae (HTV/Columbia) as pirate ship in battle with *Ciudad de Inca* off Dartmouth. Seven-week winter voyage to Caribbean via Canary Islands – successfully weathered frequent gales of force 9–11.

Marques is rigged partly as for early and partly as for the late period of the nineteenth century. With little alteration she can be authentically rigged as for the eighteenth century, or to represent a ship of almost any period.

Note: *Marques*'s owners arranged the static wreck for *Dracula* on a south Cornish beach: and staged a genuine wreck on a rocky north Cornish shore for *Jamaica Inn*.

PART ONE

TRAGEDY

1

THE DAY BEFORE
1 JUNE 1984

The very last day in which life was normal was the first day
of June 1984.

I was on a bus going from Camden to the Strand and feeling upbeat. After a lifetime of wrong turnings, things were
working out. We all make mistakes but I had repeated mine:
I chose the wrong career and compounded the error by
marrying the wrong man. Having aspired to be a writer,
instead I went on the stage and it took me twenty years to
change horses. I married for love a man who was looking for
a mother. After having two children I divorced him. Only to
take up prison-visiting as a hobby. From frying pan into fire, I
then married a man doing life for murder. When it proved a
disaster, I was the only one surprised. Forced to seek a
divorce, if only for the sake of my two teenage children, I had
to appear before a judge in Chambers as the marriage had
lasted less than three years. The judge, who was not the

stuffed shirt in wig and gown I had expected, shook his head, as if to say, 'Whatever possessed you to do something quite so daft?'

As June begins, the page has been turned and the future is looking bright. My daughter, who left school at sixteen to work in a nightclub, is learning to type. Her younger brother, having skirted A levels, is in the Caribbean, realizing his dream and competing in the Tall Ships Race. With a new agent, I am writing for television. As the bus rattles through Camden Town and swerves into Kingsway, I dare to believe things are looking up. Only one hurdle remains. After my disastrous second marriage, the Home Office were tight-lipped and the press rather too interested. For the murderer and I had written a book about our romance. Due, any day now, to be screened at BAFTA. I am not looking forward to the 'I told you so's' but otherwise the future looks rosy. Ben phoned last night from Bermuda saying they had won the trophy and that British Airways were to fly him home, gratis, for a holiday. The kindly judge, who granted my divorce, would have been pleased. After some tumultuous years, the future is looking rosy.

Pride, so they say, goes before a fall: the Greeks used to call it hubris.

2

THE FIRST DAY
3 JUNE 1984

Sunday morning. Open a bleary eye. Better get up.

I had been in a storm with Ben all night, was dry-eyed and weary. I should be in good spirits. Last night Ben phoned from Bermuda, collect as usual. Of the race, he said carelessly, 'Oh, by the way, we won.' It is six months since we saw him. After taking A levels – and deciding he'd failed – all he wanted to do was to get out to the Caribbean for the Tall Ships Race. He had been eight when I first enrolled him in sailing school, and he had once accused me of ruining his life, that he was not five. He reads voraciously, mostly Tom Sharpe, and is clearly intelligent. I must ring his dad, pass on the news. Though his father loved him he had not been the father he needed. With that, plus a bossy mother, it had not been easy for him. Sailing helped, giving him plenty of male company. We had always been close but now he wanted to show me he could stand on his own two feet. He is eighteen now: celebrated his last birthday at sea. Last night, in that phone call across the Atlantic, I'd asked – though heaven knows why as we avoid soppy talk – if he still loved me. He had said, 'Course I do, and tell the old man I love him too.' For once I had not said, 'This is costing me an arm and a leg,' and we'd talked as if there was all the time in the world. He would be home for a visit once the race was over and said, as if it was a given, he would first go to Amsterdam to see Tine, the girlfriend we had never met. He could not say exactly when he would turn up but would keep in touch. Ben is eighteen but speaks like a businessman up to his ears in appointments. It is early June: the third day of June, to be precise, and a day I will never forget. Something feels wrong. Better get up.

My daughter stayed over last night. She has found a holi-day home swap in the local paper and wants to discuss it. Some French woman in Montpelier wants to swap with someone in Hampstead. She is all fired up with the idea for the two of us. But Ben's coming home puts a spanner in the works and she is not best pleased. I have decided to take us both to Kenwood House where the azaleas will be in bloom. Put chicken in oven. Get in car. Drive up the hill to Highgate, hoping to find a compromise. At Kenwood an army of colour is on parade. Red is the order of the day and here in every shade. From the ominous purple of an aubergine to the hopeful pale pink of a baby's bottom. I cannot get last night out of my head. Ben and I had talked, for what seemed like hours. Said all there was to say. Now I ask myself, why? Shocking pink: a blaze of orange, gallant purple: the colours of a setting sun.

Drive home. Open oven. Prod chicken, which runs pink. Everything is a shade of red today. Close oven and switch on radio, tuned to LBC, and catch the tail end of a news-flash: '...a British square-rigged cutter went down in the waters off Bermuda last night...'

We freeze and our eyes lock. 'They didn't say which boat.'

'Ring LBC.'

I dial trembling. Someone says, 'Newsroom.'

As I start to ask, he cuts across me to say, 'We're up to our ears in a big news story.'

'Was it *Marques*?'

'Who is this?'

The room starts to turn. 'Ben...' I say, then stop.

Business-like, he asks, 'What's his full name?'

But I know already. I've known since last night.

He says, 'Ring the US coastguards.' I have begun to wonder if I should ring Peter and must have said some-thing as he says, 'I think you will find he already knows; it's on all the channels.' I start to shake and put down the phone. My daughter says, 'Ring Rosalie and Lew.'

This is a good idea. They are close in both senses of the word: live round the corner and I have been surrogate mum to Rosalie's Ollie since he was five. The boys are like brothers.

Lew picks up. 'Hullo.'

'Lew, Ben's boat...'

'We've just sat down to eat, can I ask Rosalie...'

'He's...' My voice breaks and Rosalie picks up: 'Shirley, what is it?'

'Ben...'

'No!'

'It's on the news. *Marques* has gone down.'

They arrive bearing coffee from the dinner table, vodka from the freezer. No one knows how to behave. Nothing prepares you for this. Rosalie says, 'Oh, Shirley' and we clutch each other. Becca looks frozen. Lew takes charge, organizes coffee, pours alcohol, marshals us. Seeing a script lying on a table he says, 'Sit down all of you, we will do a play reading.' Rosalie says faintly, 'Do a what?' and shakes her head. But Lew ploughs on, 'It will be the middle of the night over there and he'll be on a lifeboat. There'll be no news till morning.'

We do as we're told like zombies. I have gone into shock and everything seems unreal. Later, I ring LBC back and they give me the number of the US coastguards. They prove to be calm and professional 'No ma'am...not as yet...yes ma'am, you can call us any times you wish, but for sure we will call you the minute we hear anything.'

I talk to them on and off throughout the night. We read aloud. Catnap.

Then Peter rings; he is coming over.

3

THE MORNING AFTER AND AFTER THAT
4 JUNE 1984

A grey dawn. Earlier there were colours in the sky but now grey has settled in. No need for celebration in the sky when the world has changed and there is nothing to be said and nothing to be done and all we can do is to try to hang on.

Officially, we wait for news. Down at the other end of the room Peter and Lew make tea. Mugs clatter and sound seems magnified as we wait for that call, which may mean everything. The phone shrills again but when I pick up, the voice which emerges does not sound like mine.

'Hullo?'

'Mrs Bryant? Colin Seale, Race Director for the Sail Training Association. It is my job to keep you in touch with what is happening. I want to assure you that air-sea rescue have been out since first light and American coastguards are out in force, as are reconnaissance planes. If Ben is anywhere on that water we will find him'.

Behind me Rosalie mutters, 'He must be all right, he's so sensible.' But Peter and I know. I say thank you to Colin. Function but at a low level. The doorbell rings. People arrive and one of them is my brother Alan, Ben's uncle. Then Colin is on the line again and talking of the guard ship, the *Assiniboine,* and a Russian vessel called the *Cwezczerny,* both of which have been picking up survivors.

More people drift in. The phone again: this time a new voice filled with concern. A voice with a Cornish burr and as dark as treacle.

'Robin Cecil-Wright.'

'Who?'

'I am co-owner of *Marques.*'

'I thought Mark Litchfield…'

'We were partners once but no longer. Mrs Bryant, believe me there is every chance Ben will be found. Do not give up hope. Incredible things happen at sea.'

His voice comforts me. For a moment I dare to think there may yet be hope.

LBC ring. They want an interview. My brother shakes his head but I decide to do it. I ask if a presenter I know is on duty. Something has been said about not putting youngsters off going to sea and it has struck a nerve. Ben would not want that. He is free, so I say I will do it. People shake their heads, but it's my grief not theirs. Jan arrives. Jan is exactly the person you need at a time like this. She takes over, makes coffee and as more people arrive, directs them to the 'offie' saying 'Alcohol is needed' and bottles of wine begin to accumulate. Soon we shall float in a haze of alcohol. Jan, colleague, close friend, admirer of Ben, has brought a poem she wrote in the early hours. The last stanza reads:

I do believe
That impact lingers
Lasting image
Made from heroes
You, our loved one
We shall keep.
A life of thresholds
Now singing with dolphins.

The LBC guy arrives and we go up to my study. Last time we met was at some local radio station. I was publicizing a book and we talked of Ben. Now he asks, 'Ready?' takes level and we record. On air, I say that I expect my son to return, but if he should not, I will found a sailing charity in his name for disadvantaged youngsters who want to learn to sail. The LBC guy runs the tape back and nods, it's a wrap.

Downstairs the room has begun to fill up and the phone never stops. Then time starts to slip and tumble. One day melts into the next and I can no longer be sure of the order in which things happened, who was there or what anyone said. All I can say is that everything seemed unreal. You cannot mourn your dead while a search is going on so Peter and I simulated hope. But we knew Ben had gone. I had known since that night we were in a storm together. While air-sea rescue was ongoing, there was hope, or supposedly. But now, life began to assume the quality of a dream: one tinged with nightmare. I can say for certain that Peter was there much of the time. That Jan seemed there constantly and I could not have done without her. That newspapers rang and somebody answered. But as to the days, nights or the order in which things happened, I cannot be sure of anything.

David Johnston, radio producer and close friend, rings, says, 'Cookie' (my nickname to mates) but is too choked to go on. Then he blurts out the offer of a part in a radio play: 'a cough and a spit' next week. It is his way of offering comfort. David fancied Ben and my canny son, wishing not to cause offence to mum's guest, would hide when he came and re-appear in time for dessert. David offers me a part because it's all he can think of to comfort me: a gift from one actor to another. Knows it will do me good to be with chums: banish my ghosts and the spectre of Ben descending to the depths, his silky hair streaming upwards.

The noise level grows. The front door stays open; the phone never stops. Noise cushions pain. Peter goes up to the Heath to howl his grief to the skies like Lear, and I envy him for my eyes are dry. He talks of holding a memorial service at Hampstead Parish Church and asks if I mind. Mind? I am for everyone doing anything that helps. There will be no burial. What remains of my son lies at the bottom of the ocean. Then I remember I am a Jew, and ring the Rabbi at the Liberal Synagogue in St John's Wood, where Peter and I went through a marriage ceremony and I wore white lace and a veil, for all the good it did. The Rabbi says, 'Ben? My wife has been up crying all night.' Bewildered I ask, 'Why, did you know Ben?' No longer observant, I had never taken either child to a synagogue. The Rabbi explains: 'Ben was our window cleaner. Not a good window cleaner but a great talker.'

Ben had done a window-cleaning round to raise money for his voyage. The Rabbi and his wife were clients and became friends. He tells me they regularly cracked open a bottle of wine together and put the world to rights and did I know Ben was an anarchist? No, but nothing ever surprises me about Ben. He was always a law unto himself. The Rabbi confirms that he will be honoured to say Kadesh for his friend, next Saturday, that goes without saying.

Days pass; time stretches. Days and nights merge. Peter starts to organize a memorial service at Hampstead Parish Church. The vicar has offered him the use of the church on a Thursday. Peter gets orders of service printed and procures a sound system. I go to Broadcasting House to do my 'cough and spit' for David. The cast are amazed to see me and in the canteen, people stare. Newspaper pictures of the dead are all over the media. Air-sea rescue is still ongoing. In theory there is still hope but we know that it is all over bar the shouting. Calls from the press begin. I answer the first myself and say, 'Ms Cooklin is not available.' Then some bright spark in the newsroom joins the dots. It's that woman who divorced that ex-con and finally we are under siege by the press. I am upstairs when I hear the doorbell ring and Becca screaming, 'My brother is dead, don't you know? Go away!'

Having first taken relief in fantasy, seeing Ben as a hero of ancient Greece, breasting the waves, now, as reality breaks through I take to my bed, mute with pain. Late last night a letter was hand-delivered from Beryl Bainbridge, who was a close friend. As young actors we had been in rep together. Beryl and Ben enjoyed a special relationship. Wont to use nursery-type names for her friends, she always called him Ben-Ben. She is famous as a writer now. I always thought she was destined to be a painter. The letter reads: 'Shirl, I read the news in the *Evening Standard* and keep listening to the news. Ben is such a lovely, strong, resourceful boy, that I cannot believe he will not survive. Oh Shirl! When a thing like this happens it damages us all, Beryl X.'

Peter takes my car and drives to Camden Town to fetch her. Beryl walks into my bedroom and we cling together and cry. Then we get under the covers and cry some more. In between sobs, I tell her I think I am going mad as I keep seeing him as a hero of ancient Greece, bowling through the skies on his chariot. Beryl pats me like a dog, says, 'It's normal, flower, to take refuge in fantasy.' Then to distract me she says, 'Tell me again about that time Ben forgot his key and got in through the coal hole.'

'You mean when he did that commercial?'

'Yes,' says Beryl and ramps up the story. 'Didn't he breeze in and get the part over all those primped-up Italia Conti tots in their blazers?' As she speaks I seem to see him, as he was that day, an eleven-year-old, home from school at lunchtime, without permission. His mother is out and he has forgotten his key. Being of a resourceful nature, Ben gets in through the coal hole to emerge in the hall, covered in dust and cobwebs. Hearing the phone in the kitchen, he answers. A family friend called Jeannie, whose husband is a film producer, is casting a commercial for the *Sunday Times*. After a year-long print strike they want to announce the re-opening of the newspaper. Ben is their actual paperboy and Jeannie urges him to attend the audition. Ben, famously vague, looks for a pencil to take down the address but can't see one, so reckons he will remember the address (though famous for having a memory like a sieve). About to buy his first sailing dinghy, he thinks the money from a commercial would be useful so is keen as mustard to attend the audition. Back at school, he gets leave to attend the audition. But once on the bus, discovers (surprise, surprise) that he has forgotten the address after all. He appeals to the bus conductor, 'It's something to do with a Magistrate.' The conductor says, 'You want Beak Street, mate. Next stop.' Ben gets off and saunters into the lavish offices of the advertising agency.

Beryl takes up the story again. 'And didn't Ben claim he was his own agent and make up a career, on the spur of the moment?'

'Yes, told a black lie and said that he nearly played the lead in *Just William*.'

'Then did they start to audition him?'

'That's right, Ben goes into his famous bedtime "kicking-socks-into-the-air" routine, which ends with him catching the sock on his big toe. He probably looked up at them from under those ridiculously long lashes, to make sure he'd got his laugh. Not the child of two actors for nothing...' I have started to laugh now and soon we are both hysterical. 'Yes, that would have done it,' giggles Beryl.

Then she stops. 'Do you reckon Ben-Ben might have ended up an actor?'

'No chance, it was all about boats with him.'

'Pity,' she says. 'Seems ages since we were in rep, doesn't it, flower?'

'It is ages: it's over twenty years.'

Beryl pulls a comic face. 'It can't be, we're not old enough.'

Our laughter stops. Beryl changes the subject. 'Remember the time that stuck-up cow was playing Claudia and asked to borrow your gymslip as if you were ten years old?' We giggle again at the memory. Then her shoulders droop. 'Oh Shirl,' she says. 'Whatever possessed you to let him sail all those thousands of miles away!'

4

LONDON NINE
MONTHS EARLIER
SEPTEMBER 1983

'I'm goin' to the Caribbean.'

He'd entered on zephyr feet but I'd heard the front door. I knew that to argue would be to throw oil on troubled waters: I needed the skills of a Richelieu but was just his mother.

Two years ago, at fifteen, while sitting his GCSEs, it had occasionally slipped Ben's mind to turn up for the exam. Now he is halfway through A levels and the scenario is repeated. But something else is in the mix, for it is also time for the Tall Ships Race. All the big vessels have already left and Ben does not have a berth. I knew to argue would be to add fuel to his fire. My only hope was to play him at his own game. So, keeping my voice low, I ask how long he plans to be away. He had intended to respond with aggression to whatever I said. But I was being too reasonable. He makes for the door, then says grudgingly, 'I dunno.' After a pause he adds, 'Three years maybe...or forever' and then is gone before I can even draw breath.

At the time of the last Tall Ships Race he and a friend, Luke, were taken on by the skipper of the *United Friendly* and sailed from Falmouth to Portugal. There they joined vessels and crew from around the world, and he met Tine, the Dutch girlfriend we have never met. I know only that she is tall, fair, sailing-mad and they had bonded on sight. Tine was eighteen; Ben, sixteen, but mature for his age. He came home with an incipient beard and we had teased him about his 'older woman'.

Now I like to think of him having the time of his life and falling in love for the first – and as it turned out – only time in his life. Only after his death did I learn from Alex that Ben had almost been swept overboard on the voyage back. There had been an almighty row over seamanship with the skipper. When they reached port, Luke decided to apologize. Ben, uncompromising as ever, refused. Now Luke is on board *United Friendly* again and Ben is out in the cold. With time running out he scans yachting magazines, writes a long letter to the skipper of *The Eye of the Wind*, now in Australia. *Marques*, the boat he first sailed at fifteen, in Spain, has already left. His options are dwindling fast and time is running out. With A levels banished to the dustbin of history, Ben decides if he can get out to the Canaries, he stands a better chance of picking up a berth. He knows a guy who plans to sail there on a 28-foot

Twister and offers to help with preparation. They go down every weekend to work on the boat and plan to leave in early September. I buy him a red Helly Hansen storm-coat. My brother Alan gives him a Swiss Army Knife as an early birthday present, not the oiled seaman's socks that Ben had modestly requested.

In September, as they are about to leave, the boat develops engine trouble. Soon it will be too late. But they are ready in the nick of time and we make our farewells. Ben has been spending summers on boats since he was eight, making voyages since fourteen. It is just one more setting-off: one more parting, one more adventure. Later we learn they encountered a storm in the Bay of Biscay and rode it out by staying below and eating fruitcake. In the Canaries they part company. Ben, set on going to the Caribbean, must find a vessel to cross the Atlantic. Meantime, he lives in a run-down hotel, existing on tomatoes and grapes. With money and hope running out, his sister mounts a rescue and flies out with a boyfriend. They hire a car, drive him all over the island until they find a Frenchman with a catamaran who needs crew. 'Think of me,' writes Ben '… as I start the long trek across the Atlantic.'

Two weeks pass, with no word. I ring Peter saying I think it is time to ring the British Consul. He agrees but that afternoon a letter arrives from Ben, chirpy as ever.

LES SAINTES, 8 January 1984. 'I'm now in the Caribbean…' he writes in his spidery hand, '…the crossing was quite hard because the automatic pilot wasn't working and I had to steer six hours a day, two in the morning, one in the afternoon, three at night. My feet and back were tired until the day after we dropped anchor. The most exhausting time was the last night, because me and another guy steered for ten hours, half an hour on, half an hour rest, though I don't know why Michel, the skipper, spent the whole night lying down in the saloon, smoking. He proved rather strange while at sea, hot tempered and difficult about food, but I'm staying for at least one month. This will be no great crusade or suffrage because he is completely different once the anchor has been dropped. Also, he can't sail the boat on his own, so he needs me and consequently is now careful not to push me too far.

'A few days ago, on Dominica he exploded after I'd been to Roseau to try and extend our visas and when I returned to the boat without the extensions, he went mad. It is supposed to be the Captain who goes to the immigration but he wasn't prepared to travel the thirty-five miles or, for that matter, tell me that I was supposed to go in and say, 'I am the Captain', brandishing a passport with a photograph depicting a very young-looking face. Anyway, while he was hurling abuse at me I decided I'd had enough and that it was time to say goodbye. Fortunately for us both he realized this and shut up. We went and had a drink and he began to talk about the possibility of chartering (necessity£?) and that then he would pay me. We are going to all the other islands of any interest so there will be no shortage of boats. It's difficult for me to go on my own because of immigration problems. So, it's best I am patient and wait to see what will happen. This is no great sacrifice as it's more relaxed on board at the moment and isn't costing me anything. And there is the endless sun, beaches lined with palm trees, coconuts on the ground, calypsos, bananas and that kind of thing.

'I left Monsieur Michel's boat in Guadeloupe after an extremely boring time. Many, many times I had thought of just leaving, even though I had no place to go and not enough money to support myself. But each time I changed my mind by the next morning.

'For the final decision I was greatly encouraged by certain liquid substances. That night there was a big American charter boat alongside. Previously, in the morning the owner had borrowed our hose and, in the evening, he asked if he could borrow it one more time. As a gesture of gratitude, he chucked over a bottle of rum, Michel was out of sight bullshitting to a fellow creeping frog and due to his absence, I drank most of the bottle. This kind of roused my spirits, causing me to make the final decision. I already knew of a Norwegian boat, heading up to Tortola and Florida so I decided to go and see the owner next day.

'I went to see the skipper and all was fixed up, I swapped boats the following day. I made one proviso that we stop in Antigua. The reason I gave was that I needed a visa for the US but my reasons, left unspoken, were that I had an idea that the China Clippers were in Antigua, plus if they wouldn't have me I might find another boat, more to my advantage.

'The day after I arrived in Antigua I was offered a job on *Marques*. At last I had made it. I couldn't sleep that night I was so overjoyed and decided to tell the owner the following morning. But next morning things went very stale. He made a hell of a fuss, saying I'd promised to stay aboard until the boat was sold, which was complete and utter shit. Anyway, I packed my bags and took them over to the *Marques*. But there was a problem: when I first went on his boat he made me leave a deposit of a hundred pounds to ensure I would cause him no expense when I left and now would not hand this over until I was signed off his crew list. It is the immigration, who do this in Antigua and this public body is run by Sergeant King, infamous all over the Caribbean for his unjust dictatorship.

'Anyway, he went into Sergeant King's office and requested for me to be signed off one crew list and placed on another. Immediately Sergeant King said, 'Right, he'll have to fly off the island.' I tried to speak and was told to shut up. Sergeant King's policy is to speak only to Captains. Consequently, I had a man fighting my case, who was trying to get me to stay with him and saying so to Sergeant King. I felt lost in a state of hopelessness. I'd come up against a brick wall, tasted what banana republics are all about. The conclusion was that I'd have to sail to Tortola with the Norwegian and then fly back to Antigua airport where the captain of *Marques* would take me through immigration. If you don't quite understand the sense in this whole scenario, it is probably because it is totally absurd.

'I retrieved my bags from *Marques* and returned to *Top Lady*, totally despondent. Next day, just before we went back to immigration for clearance to leave, I found a guy who wanted to go to Tortola. If I could persuade him to come along then I could get off at the next island north without any fuss. This would save time and money. It turned out that he too needed a visa for the US so couldn't leave until Monday. Because of this, the plan was that we'd sail to Saint Martin, the next island up north, and once he arrived I could leave for Antigua.

'Now the owner had the cheek to think that I must wait until his new crew arrived and, failing his arrival, sail to Tortola with him. I don't know why. All this made me even more angry, having a person I don't even know, and who wasn't paying me, attempting to run my life. Of course, I was going to get off in Saint Martin but I really didn't want to do it on the sligh [sic].

'Though infuriated and frustrated by the situation, it was fairly sorted out and after the mammoth discussion the three of us went to get clearance to leave. It was Sergeant King's day off and another guy was there so I asked, in passing, if he'd sign me off. He said okay and that was that.

'So now I'm on *Marques*, still in Antigua, and having a really great time. At the moment we are doing 'Day Charter', which is hard work but fun because we get to sail the ship three days a week, also the air is fresher out at sea. At the beginning of April, we are heading up to Puerto

Rico to join the Tall Ships Race to Quebec via Bermuda and Halifax, Nova Scotia.

'After the race Air Canada will give me a free flight home. So, if it all comes off it should be fantastic. Love, Ben.'

SIX WEEKS LATER, 24 April 1984, ANTIGUA. 'Dear Mum and all, I have been writing, you are definitely not forgotten, however the Antiguan Post Office is quite unreliable, particularly when it comes to outgoing mail. Whatever, I'm having a great time.

'Our little American Charter business will be wound up soon and then we are off. The Antiguan yachting scene is a bit of a merry-go-round and seething with money but we, the ominous men of the square-riggers, stand out as something different. I think it is a plastic society, but still find plenty to enjoy. Apparently, we have a reputation that spreads all the way to Miami: raucous English pirates, raising havoc, a bit silly really but quite amusing all the same.

I know you were all hoping that I would be accepted as crew. There really wasn't any need to worry. Nick Dutton in the office is 3,000 miles away and has little to do with the day-to-day running of the ships. Furthermore, quite a few of the crew have left recently, leaving a gap that I easily filled. We are becoming quite a crack crew as we get so much sailing. Who knows who will win the Tall Ships Race? But one thing is sure, *Marques* will have a good crew. I managed to get the hang of the three miles of running rigging in about a week and by now it is completely understood. When we are chartering we can have all sails set before we leave harbour, having weighed anchor and stowed the mooring ropes.

'We are getting a reputation for being the real sailors in English harbour and because of this "image" me and another guy called Bobby Cooper have been offered a job on an enormous and immensely expensive yacht that just cruises around the world. By the time we will be needed (about six months' time) the boat will be in Australia, where two old China Clipper guys are leaving. By the way the pay starts at 800 US dollars per month, with paid holidays and airfares of course. So, if I leave *Marques* in Canada, who knows what may happen – Canadian Airways can fly me home and the owner of *Aspasia Alfa* can fly me to Australia, but enough of that or you'll start to think I've run away for good.'

Ben's letters continued, spasmodic but lighthearted. In May, sailing vessels of all nationalities and types converged on Bermuda for the 1984 Tall Ships Race to Halifax, Nova Scotia. Ben is taken on as crew by First Mate, Charlie Lanyon. At last he is back with his mates. *Marques* takes five days to cover the 600 miles from San Juan to Bermuda. As sleeker and faster boats disappear over the horizon, the crew decide to forget about the race and enjoy the sail. When they amble into Bermuda harbour, one of the last boats to arrive, they are astonished to be greeted by cries of 'You've won!' and think this is the funniest thing they have ever heard. They sail to Georgetown for refuelling, then motor back into Hamilton and moor, stern to quayside, alongside the rather grand Princess Hotel. Andy had maintenance work to do on the engine and batteries to fill, and a new cylinder to install on the outboard motor. Ben, in charge of the rubber dinghy as usual, ferried stores back and forth. As a child, when we had camped in Devon, he ferried other children in his rubber dinghy at Hope Cove and was known as 'The Volga Boatman'. They are all in high spirits. Bobby, in a mad mood, climbs to the top of the mast of the *Simón Bolívar* and does the return trip slipping all the way down the backstay. Watching officers are not impressed and tell him in no uncertain terms that he ought to have climbed down the way he went up.

Meantime, Andy, Gillie and Ben wander round town together. They bump into Pete, who had gone off on his own. Then all four got lost and must ask a policeman the way. Back on the quayside they are just in time to see *The Eagle*, a big American vessel, come in alongside. The quay is 20 feet wide and there is not enough room for the gangplank. They find it hilarious when the young Americans solve the problem by taking up the railings. Then the *Marques* crew go off to attend the prize-giving ceremony. All except Andy, busy getting his engine ready. The others return, whooping with joy, calling out to Andy to come and see the trophy. A picture is taken which shows Ben and Bobby, immaculate in 'whites', posed with Carl in blue jeans. But while Bobby and Carl smile for the camera, Ben in the middle wears his 'this photo is being taken against my will' face. Then they persuade Andy to take off his overalls and go with them to the yacht club. Laughing, they make their way along a series of pontoons.

Next day they are hard at work making preparations for departure. Barefoot, scruffy, they amble back and forth through the elegant foyer of the Princess Hotel, carrying gas canisters, spare parts and supplies. On Thursday night the last of the paying passengers come aboard. Ian Brims, a British journalist who emigrated to Canada, told his wife Nina this was something he wanted to do before he was too old. There were two American ASTA counsellors, Sue Howell and Stu Gillespie, and an older couple, Jack and Thelma Heath, a young woman called Andrea Lee and the fifteen-year-old son of a millionaire, Tommy Le Bel. There were also four hefty young Americans, Cliff and James McAleer and Bill Barnhardt and Jay Ash.

Sometime during those weeks after the disaster, Ben's friend Jason came to see us. He told us about meeting Ben in the Caribbean and described his own feelings on seeing land, after days and days on the ocean. 'It was amazing to arrive at this tiny island in the middle of nowhere, after days of seeing nothing but water. That is the strange thing about sailing; you are always waiting for the next port. But when you arrive, you want to get sailing again. I could hardly believe it when I bumped into Ben on the dockside. I'd been away a few weeks, Ben for nine months. It must have been even stranger for him. It was a shock, so far from home, to meet someone you knew. He had a little rubber dinghy and took me back to see his ship, *Marques*. There was a really ancient smell about her as they tar everything. Now, the smell of tar brings back that moment when I bumped into Ben. He looked like a buccaneer or a pirate. Tanned, his hair sun-bleached and one gold earring. He was wearing some old khaki army pants and really looked the part.'

Jason told us Ben showed him over *Marques* and introduced him to Andy, who was mad keen to join Canada Maritime. It was a running gag that Ben would get Andy to do favours against an introduction. Jason took them back to see his ship and Ben met up with Luke again. 'I didn't see much of Ben in Bermuda…' says Luke, '…there was a lot going on and I had a girlfriend who took up most of my time. I figured we'd meet up and exchange news when we reached Halifax. I thought there would be all the time in the world, once we reached Halifax.'

After they reached Bermuda the days were spent preparing for departure. They were ready to leave when they hit a snag: the sister boat, the *Inca*, captained by Mark Litchfield himself, had bent her steering shaft and so arrived late. With no time to fit a new rudder, everything was in question. Finally, permission was given for *Inca* to start the race late but the organizers insisted *Marques* must leave with the others.

On the last day, Ben went into Hamilton to re-stock the ship's bar: that same ship's bar later to be so hotly denied during the Inquiry. He takes along an American woman, Gypsy Vanderveer, to show her the ropes as she is to do the same chore on *Inca*, and as we already know, Ben also found time to ring me. But suddenly the weather changed.

5

HEATHROW AIRPORT
8 JUNE 1984

On Friday 8 June, through a haze of heat and petrol fumes, we take the motorway to Heathrow. Yesterday, Colin Seale phoned to say air-sea rescue was being called off. 'But I want to reassure you no stone was left unturned.'

It is eight days now but feels like an eternity.

'What happens now?'

'We are winding down. Tomorrow I will fly home with the survivors.'

Is that it? Can a life end with so little ceremony? One moment that life mattered so much an air-sea rescue was in operation with American coastguards on lookout, guard ships searching and the entire world media focused. Must this end with a two-minute phone call? I want to meet the young people who were his friends. Learn something of that time when he was so far away. Ben was on the threshold of life. He was my son, my much-loved son. It is not just I who have lost him: the world has. At seventeen Ben had joined Greenpeace, long before it became fashionable. From the Rabbi I had learnt he was an anarchist. In theory, I know what that means but in practice I am not so sure. I want to meet the friends who shared his adventuring. Such a hopeful young life cannot end in a phone call with the careless words, 'We are winding down.' So I ask, 'Could I not meet them?' Those friends Ben spent his last days with? I would like to learn something of those months since he left home. Is it wrong; is it asking too much?' There is silence. Then he says, with the hint of a frog in his throat, 'Mrs Bryant, forgive me, I did not mean to sound abrupt. Of course his friends will be honoured to meet you. Let me see what I can arrange?'

I had spoken without thinking. I knew Ben was gone from the moment I heard those words from the LBC newsreader. But there is a difference between knowing and facing facts. Yesterday, people were assuring me there was still hope. Now there is nothing, not even a grave I can visit. I want more. I need more. I want to meet the friends he sailed with.

Now we are driving to Heathrow. Yesterday, it seemed a good idea, now I'm not so sure. At the Atlantic Gate we meet up with Rosina and John Messer-Bennetts, parents of Pete who died. John Adams, a previous *Marques* skipper, has brought his wife Elizabeth who proves to be a woman of sterling qualities. There is also a tall, fair girl who says, 'Call me Mungo, everyone does.' She was the cook on *Inca* and had been flown home for medical reasons. Later I would learn that the term 'medical' can have other meanings. One person definitely missing is the mother of Gillie Shaughnessy, the ship's cook on *Marques*. Mrs Shaughnessy has sent a message, saying she is too upset to attend. Can she think we are not grieving? My idea was to help parents, not young survivors. But as things turned out, they needed this meeting as much as anyone. Imagine being eighteen and having to step off a plane to meet the parents of your dead comrade. After all those hours in a lifeboat, thinking you were about to drown? All we had was solidarity and clinging together. In Mrs Shaughnessy's place, there is a stocky, fair-haired Scot, who seems more upset than anyone, but turns out to be father to Bobby, one of the two survivors. Someone is missing. I was surprised that no one was there from the race, since 19 people lost their lives.

It is hot, airless, stifling and there is nowhere to sit. We have been told to wait here and don't like to move. After a while, feeling unsteady, Becca and I sit on the grimy airport floor. Then our escort arrives – a brisk young woman in a blue uniform who gathers us up, saying sorry for the wait and could we follow in twos and threes to avoid attracting attention from the waiting press. We are heading beyond customs. There, a lounge has been made available: somewhere we can meet in privacy to greet the young survivors. Colin Steele and his charges will come directly from the plane. Other survivors are still in Bermuda or else have returned to the US. Our guide hands out passes and leads us into an underground tunnel, while chattering away non-stop into her walkie-talkie.

Suddenly, everyone seems to have vanished and I am alone. My arm is gripped in a vice and questions are fired at me like bullets from a gun by a small, olive-skinned man in khaki who brandishes something which looks alarmingly like an AK-47 rifle 'Who are you?' he barks. 'Tell me your name. Now!' My throat closes in panic. I see myself locked in some small room with no way out. 'Answer me!' he shouts. Then our escort re-appears to gather me up. I am still shaking when we reach the lounge, where we stand around, bewildered. Then a commotion occurs at the door and a man, who turns out to be Colin Seale, enters shepherding two young men. One has platinum curls and looks barely fifteen. The other is dark and his eyes stare as if he is in shock. That must be Andy Freeman, the 'young sparky' who was alone in a lifeboat for eight hours, believing himself to be the only survivor. Both look bewildered. I wonder now if this was such a good idea.

They are kitted out, incongruously, in brand-new clothes, gifted by well-wishers in Bermuda as everything they owned lies on the ocean floor. Andy wears grey slacks and a navy jacket. Bobby is resplendent in white slacks and a jacket that would do credit to an Admiral, the grandeur of his outfit belied by his worried little face. He looks twelve. Both hold themselves stiffly, like army cadets, braced for an ordeal. I advance towards the fair boy like some woman at a cocktail party with my hand out, saying,

'I am Ben's mum; did you know him?' He looks at me from his sad grey eyes and says, 'I am Bobby and Ben was my brother.' I feel very foolish. Then we fall weeping into each other's arms.

Andy, silent and watchful, reminds me sharply of Ben. As if at a stroke, ice is broken and everyone starts talking at once. Elizabeth dispenses coffee and hands out tranquilizers like sweets. The dads bring out hip-flasks to lace the coffee with something stronger. The ordeal has become a party and, as with all good parties, everyone talks at once. Bobby opens his brand-new suitcase, gets down on his hands and knees to bring out sheaves of coloured photographs of *Marques*, which he distributes with largesse. I am reminded of those men who used to stand on the pavement outside Selfridges before the war, selling novelties out of a suitcase – one eye on the punters and the other watching out for 'the boys in blue'.

Next, Bobby switches to letters, which he dispenses to Pete's mother, Rosina and to me, from crewmates and the sister ship *Inca*. Emotion runs high as Rosina and I open our letters. They are from both sets of crews, or what is left of them. Some are carefully composed. 'You can in every way be truly proud of Ben and I think I know that he was doing to the last, the things in life his heart told him to.' Others are scribbled on a page torn from a notebook. '*Marques* was a warm ship, full of love, Ben only made it warmer.' Another begins, 'Dear Ben's Mum, I'm sorry I don't know your name…' Yet another is addressed 'to Ben's family' and begins, 'Dear Mr and Mrs Ben, I am sorry I don't know your names, but Ben was a very good friend of mine.'

With tongues loosened by tots of brandy, reminiscences begin. Mungo says, 'I was making pastry in the galley one day when Ben decided to help. He had no sooner begun rolling it out than all the others piled in and started fooling around. It turned into a scrum. There was flour all over the shop and blobs of pastry everywhere.' An image from the past hits me: Ben, five or six, serious, sits at the kitchen table cutting out mince pies. Suddenly, his mood changes and mercurial he lobs a grey mauled lump of pastry at the ceiling.

Stories are recounted. The first is from John Adams, about when he was captain. 'Charlie Lanyon, as First Mate, was a strict disciplinarian and when he said jump they all jumped pronto. One day he tells Ben, who's in charge of the rubber duck, to ferry guests to the harbour. Before Charlie can finish his sentence Ben leaps into the rubber boat and heads fast for the shore. The guests he was supposed to ferry look gobsmacked. The rest of us have begun to shout and jeer. Arriving on shore Ben ties up, looks around for his passengers. By now everyone on board is hysterical with laughter. Charlie yells, 'Come back you idiot!' Ben catches on, jumps into the rubber duck and shoots back to catcalls of derision. As he comes alongside he says, rather sheepishly, 'I think I may have got it a little bit wrong.' Everyone, including the passengers, is now hysterical.

A memory surfaces.

'Ben, where is it?'

'You never said.'

'Yes, I did.'

'Well, I never heard you.'

'Exactly! You weren't listening, were you?'

Bobby is patient when I question him about those last months. Did Ben eat fish and where did they do their washing? I seem to hear Ben saying, 'Mum, what have you done with my jeans! Those are the ones I'm wearing.' The last lines of a poem he wrote at fifteen echo in my head:

Yes, I enjoyed life
A bit short though.

Did he know? Was he called away?

Then it is time to part. Becca, frail in a pink cotton dress, is hugged by her new 'brothers'. But, as if the wind had changed, suddenly there is a new plan. We are not ready to part it seems and it has been decided Ron and Bobby will come back with us to Grafton Road (though God knows where everyone will sleep) until after the memorial. Andy, of course, must go home to Liverpool to see his anxious parents but will return. Beds are made up anywhere there is space. All that matters is being together. For me, it was as if it was a last sighting of Ben, never one to be left out if a party was in the offing. He was there – he must be, he had to be. It was just that the others could not see him.

6

COMING TO TERMS
LONDON, JUNE 1984

We are upstairs in my workroom at the back of the house, Bobby and I. Becca is spending the evening with a friend. Peter and Ron are down in the garden getting half-cut. Bobby wants to talk. I am not entirely sure I want to hear what he wants to tell me, but he is only eighteen and had to watch his best friend die. Besides which, for the moment, I am in locus parentis, with his own mother in Scotland.

Below, in the garden, the two dads, Peter and Ron carouse. We hear a laugh: a bottle placed on an iron table. Bobby asks, 'Did Ben tell you about that job we got on a big Australian yacht? It was going to be hundred dollars a week and our airfares paid.'

'Yes, that last night when he rang.'

Bobby starts to weep. 'Why did it have to happen, why?'

To distract him, I ask him to tell me about leaving Halifax. His voice becomes dreamy.

'We were moored outside the Princess Hotel. Ben and me, we came ashore in his dingy, the rubber duck. There was this red carpet inside and posh people were having lunch…' – he stops as if visualizing it – '…and a pianist in a white jacket, like in the movies.'

'How were you two dressed?'

He giggles. 'We were covered in tar and kept running in and out with our muddy feet. People gawped at us, as if we were wild animals.'

'Was Ben wearing his khaki army pants?' I ask, needing to visualize him.

'Course, he always wore them. We were both covered in mud and tipsy.' He giggles again.

'What, in the middle of the day?'

'Ben had been out buying booze for the bar and we'd done some sampling…' An image of the two teenagers hits me: both blond as angels and scruffy as down-and-outs. '…Ben remembered he had to meet someone.'

'Oh, who was that?'

'Some hippie American woman with a nutty name…' he jeers '…Gypsy Vanderveer. Ben was in charge of the bar on *Marques* and this woman had been told to take over on *Inca*. Ben had to show her the ropes cos she didn't have a clue….' He stops, remembering the moment: '…only Ben didn't want to go. He said, "S'pose I'd better."'

Bobby's eyes fill again with tears and I say hastily, 'Tell me about sailing out of Hamilton harbour.'

He wipes his eyes on a sleeve. 'There wasn't a cloud in the sky. It was how people imagine sailing. You know, all glittering water and gulls going mad. The quayside was packed. Everyone cheering. We had all sails set for the cameras and there were little kids waving flags. The crew of that Royal Navy vessel, the *Assiniboine*, were waving too and an American photographer was rushing about clicking her camera. She tried to make me, Ben and Carl pose with the trophy. When she said smile, Ben pulled a face. You know Ben. He said, "You two can be monkeys if you want but leave me out of it." When we were about a mile out the sky suddenly went dark and a great dollop of rain fell on my head. Everyone started yelling. Denis was screaming to take down sail and that photographer woman was telling Stu, our skipper, that some guys had promised to pick her up but hadn't showed. Stu said to stay on board but she kept shaking her head. The wind was getting up. Then a speedboat zoomed up. She ran to the rail and yelled. We all cheered when she jumped overboard. Then the weather changed. A really cold wind blew up and it got choppy. Trainees were hanging over the side throwing up and Denis, our First Mate, said to put on life jackets and go below. At six bells, everyone who was not "on watch" went below to eat. Andy was feeling sick so he went below to lie on his bunk.'

'Where was Ben?'

'Probably below. He was doing the eight to midnight with Denis, so would have been getting ready. Then Denis and our skipper got into conference. It was getting rougher by the minute. They decided to reduce sail. Around 11.30 Andy came back. He had put on his boiler suit and was looking better. Ben came off watch and someone, I think it was Denis, said to give his safety harness to a trainee.'

With ice in my veins, I realize this must be the life jacket I had bought to keep him safe.

Bobby has started to sob. A terrible sound. I say, 'That's enough, stop,' but he insists. 'I must tell you everything. You've a right to know. Later on Ben and I got into our bunks. At 2 a.m. Denis came down to wake us and said Pete should go aloft too and we should take down one of the sails. It was a real job in that wind. Then the three of us sat on the yard arm for a smoke. It was quieter now and the ship was running well…How could I know it was the last time I would ever see Ben?'

Wrapping my arms around him, I say over and over, 'It was not your fault; it was not your fault, Bobby; none of this was your fault!'

Gradually the crying tails off and finally stops. Down below, from the two dads, comes the sound of muffled laughter. I say, 'That's enough now.'

But Bobby won't have it. 'No, let me finish, I want to. I knew something was going to happen so stayed on deck as Phil took over the wheel. It was raining hard so Andy went to put on wet weather gear and came back to hang over the rail and watch the sea boil. All of a sudden, without any warning, the ship began to keel over. It was slow at first, then it accelerated. Suddenly she was down in the water with her mast and sails lying flat. I saw Andy let go of the poop rail and fall into the sea and found myself tangled up in the rigging. She was sinking fast. Then I was down in the saloon and all the lights were on, as if they were having a party. I thought I must be dead. Then I began floating upwards. There must have been an air bubble in my oilskins. Next I was on the surface choking and gasping for breath. My throat felt like sandpaper. I knew I must jump in and swim for my life. Then a life raft appeared and I clambered in. When I looked back, to where the ship had been, there was nothing; nothing at all. It was…'

Bobby shivers. 'There were nine of us in the dinghy and Sue Howell, our navigator, was swimming towards us when a giant wave heaved up and she disappeared. Phil was suddenly violently sick. Then I saw another life raft and thinking Ben might be in it, I strapped on a life-line and swam to her. But there was no one so I towed her back. Phil and I decided to tie the two rafts together and fired a parachute flare. It fizzled into the sea. With only one left we tied it to a paddle and were hoisting it up when we saw sails coming through the mist. It was a Polish vessel, the *Zawisza Czerny*. Crew began to drag us aboard and we saw a lifeboat with Andy in it. Thinking he was the only survivor, he was in shock. Somehow we managed to drag him aboard and sent up an almighty cheer.'

With his grim story told, Bobby seemed calmer, but now there was a new concern: getting in touch with Ben's girlfriend. Ben, typically organised, had left me the addresses of all his friends, but not that of his Dutch girl-friend, Tine, who lived in Amsterdam. Ron suggested asking the police. They contacted colleagues in Amsterdam, and now having her mother's phone number, with some trepidation, I ring and ask, 'Am I speaking to Mrs Joustra?'

She says without any trace of accent, 'Please tell me you are the mother of Benjamin.'

'Mrs Joustra, what a blessing your English is so good. Can I ask if Tine knows about Ben?'

'Yes and she is inconsolable. I am so relieved to hear from you. I have been at my wits' end to know what to do.'

'Did you ever meet Ben?'

'We were hoping to after the race. Tine and Ben had something planned.'

'So Ben told me so in his last phone call. I am sad to have never met her.'

'It is the same for me. I was thinking perhaps to bring Tine over.'

'She can stay with me. You may be sure I will look after her.'

'Then I will bring her. Take the boat-train to Victoria station and bring her to you by taxi. Tine says you live near Hampstead.'

'Sort of, but it's more Gospel Oak.'

'I can drop her off and keep the same taxi to go back to the station.'

They came the next day. Mrs Joustra got out of the taxi. We exchanged a few words, then she got back inside and Tine got out. Together we waved her mother off; then went into the house together. It was for us both as if something of Ben had returned. Tine's arrival was a balm I could never have imagined. As to where we all slept that night: Bobby had the living room sofa, while Becca shared Ben's old room with my two New Zealand lodgers. As for the rest of us, Peter went back every evening to his girlfriend's house. Tine and I shared my double bed and poor Ron drew the short straw and slept on the bathroom floor. Right from the start Tine and I were easy with each other. She told me how they first met two years ago, at the last Tall Ships Race in Portugal. Tine was on deck, doing a really complicated sailor's knot, when she heard someone say, 'Wow' and turned to come face to face with Ben. For both of them it had been love at first sight.

Looking back, that week seems like a golden age. The fact there was no going back, that Ben would never return, had not yet sunk in. It was as if he were just away sailing. We became a tight group for whom, being together and being surrounded, diluted the pain of reality. It was June and London was enjoying the mother of all heatwaves. We drifted in a haze of alcohol without any sense of the passage of time. We ate and drank, laughed and cried, as if in some sort of buffer zone. The world, seen through a haze of alcohol, looked a different place. One day seemed to flow into the next. For that short space, we became an entity, with only one focus. It was a no man's land of flow-ers, wine and sunshine. We were six but when the Vickies (my two New Zealand lodgers) joined us, we became eight sometimes. We were all high on the solidarity of being together. We knew it must soon end, but for as long as we were together the future was a tomorrow that might never come.

It was the longest week I can ever remember. There were moments when reality broke through. Bobby began to talk about the memorial service. He wanted to buy flowers for his friend and I promised to take him early that morning to Queen's Crescent Market. Then we resumed the drinking, the drifting and sitting under umbrellas. I wanted to stop time and for nothing more to ever happen. I did not want to face the emptiness I knew must come. When that week was over, I would have to face facts: begin some sort of new life, one without Ben in it. But for as long as the six (or the eight) of us were together, in that bubble of wine, sunshine and solidarity, there was only the dust as the cars went past to remind us of the real world.

On the Saturday I went to the Liberal Jewish Synagogue in St John's Wood to join in intoning the traditional prayers for the dead. In this I was much comforted by the knowl-edge that the Rabbi's prayers were personal because Ben had been his friend. Finally, the day of the memorial service at Hampstead Parish Church was upon us. That morning the house was alive with young voices: calling out variously to borrow a hairbrush, or to say, 'Have mine.'

Black clothes were banned. We would celebrate Ben's young life with the distaff side in dresses in the sweet-pea hues of early summer and the boys in their everyday jeans. True to my promise I took Bobby to the market to buy flowers for his friend. As they were being wrapped, someone called out 'Ben!' We both turned in shock, only to see that 'Ben' was a black Labrador.

At Hampstead Parish Church we were greeted by children from Ben's old primary school singing 'The Lord is My Shepherd'. A series of tributes followed. Becca went tremulously to the microphone, to introduce her brother's favourite piece of music, Led Zeppelin's 'Stairway to Heaven'. She told us how he used to listen with his cat Violet on his lap. Ben's cousin Lisa played the oboe. Bobby read 'Jesus' Farewell' to his friends. My brother Alan, Ben's uncle, provided a note of humour as he recalled that his own son, Danny, had taken to calling his cousin Fungus – an allusion to Ben's rejection of baths and freshwater in favour of the salt variety.

After the service Peter and I emerged from the gloom; more a couple that day than we had ever been. Half the BBC were there with a mix of family and close friends. Ben, during his short life, had touched many. I had received letters from people who met him in Bermuda and teachers from his sixth-form college. We stood blinking in the June sunshine, thinking that this could not be happening. Then we went back to Grafton Road for a feast, where, as a nod to Ben's preferences I served the sort of peasant food he had loved. My sister-in-law Fiz had baked a whole ham and I had made a giant potato salad glistening with olive oil, frosty with sea-salt. There were strawberries and a chocolate roulade. Out in the back garden, bottles of wine stood in buckets of ice. As the day waned, younger spirits took off for the pub to let off steam while the golden oldies sat on the floor to reminisce. When night fell and everyone had gone, Sal, one of my closest friends, came straight from playing at an outer-London theatre. We sat out in the dark, remembering a recent visit to an Indian palmist. We had taken his predictions seriously, but I insisted that he had been wrong in seeing a large gathering for me. I had interpreted it as a celebration for Ben's homecoming. But Sal reminded me that in India they call death a celebration.

Finally, I am alone to wake in the morning and lie inert, watching sunlight filter through the lace curtains and form patterns on the wall. This acts as some sort of sedative and prevents me from thinking. But I have begun to sense that Ben is around and is trying to tell me something. Can it have to do with that giant wind, which supposedly overturned the boat? I decide I am doing no good to anyone lying here and get up to wander the familiar streets. Those were the streets where I once used to wheel Ben in his pram. Now I find myself remembering him, not as the young man who set sail for the other side of the world, but the baby and the toddler he once was. I keep thinking I can see him just ahead of me, but when he turns it is always some other small boy, pulling at his mother's hand as Ben used to pull at mine. Hearing the chime of an ambulance bell, as it bowls through the streets, I rejoice, as now it can never be Ben. Nothing can hurt him ever again.

I walk without purpose, unable still to grasp that I will never see him again. I keep remembering him as an infant, who was safe at my side. Or the small boy he became. I can hear him saying fiercely, 'No, I won't!' to some little blonde cutie of three as she edged round the front door to ask if Benjie could come out to play. He always refused and would say scornfully, as the door closed behind her, 'Her and her dolly hair!'

But the time I like most to recall is when Ben was two-and-a-bit and had a partner-in-crime. Her name was Belinda, but to Ben she was Blim-Blim. Both being too young for nursery, her mother and I did a toddler-watch together. We were once in Blim-Blim's mother's kitchen, when we caught the tail-end of a conversation. The infants were next door playing in Blim-Blim's bedroom. She seemed to be asking for something, which Ben seemed unwilling to concede. We began to pay attention. 'Oh please, Benjie, say that you will.' Ben, small but no push-over, insists, 'No, I won't!' and that would seem to be the end of it. But Belinda is not about to give up and redoubles her efforts. 'Oh please, Benjie, please…' she begs, '…say that you will.'

Ben digs his toes in but suddenly tires of the argument. For if push comes to shove, Ben, just like his father, will in the end always opt for a quiet life. So, finally he capitulates, saying, 'Oh, awe white then, I will mawwy you.'

Blim-Blim's mother and I are in stitches.

As Ben grew up he did not give up so easily. He developed early an aversion to authority and must have been eleven, having recently started at the comprehensive school on Haverstock Hill, when I had a call from the Deputy Head. The Headmaster there was an easy-going man but his Deputy, an ex-prison officer, was feared by all pupils with the exception of Ben. I never did find out what he had said. But Ben, who loved a challenge, had presumably locked horns with the Dep. For one day the phone rang and I was startled to hear the Dep, addressing me as 'Missus Bryant…' Then, making the most of all three syllables he said, '…Ben-ja-min was spectacularly rude to me today.' I managed to stifle a laugh and said soothingly, 'Oh, Mr Ellis, I am sure Ben meant no disrespect.' I decided not to ask Ben what he had said. It seemed safer not to know.

However, the Dep was not the only member of staff to query Ben's style. I once had a run-in with his Maths teacher, a kind and gentle man from Pakistan. For Ben, as for me before him, Maths was a closed book. Once, at a parents' evening, I asked this teacher if he would give Ben extra Maths coaching. He smiled sadly and recounted the following story. Recently, while trying to explain some Maths problem to Ben, the latter had picked up his chair, turned it around in such a fashion as to present his backside, broadside on, to his teacher and sat down. Not for nothing had the Rabbi told me that Ben was an anarchist. He never did anything by halves.

But the stories I prefer to remember are the quaint things he said when he was small. Like most second children, he relied at first on his sister to interpret the world and must have been three or four, when one day at the tea table, he said quite seriously, 'I should like my bread to be painted with jam.'

Once he decided to speak, he was away. Words fascinated Ben, but he would only speak if he had something to say and would always choose his words with care. He could, on occasion, take what seemed an inordinate amount of time to marshal his thoughts. But if we complained about the long wait between sentences, he would explain, 'It takes a long time 'cos I have to think.'

This morning, I decide it is high time to pull myself together. I must resume my daily swim on the Heath before a visit to Queen's Crescent Market just down the road. Today being a Thursday, the market will now be in full swing. Suddenly, it feels urgent to banish the dreams, ghosts and memories. What I need is a session of down-to-earth banter with Jack, my favourite greengrocer stall holder.

Jack, greets me, as if it was yesterday. 'All right?'

He knows about Ben. Everyone does. It was in all the nationals and there was a long piece in the *Ham & High*.

'What you been up to?'

I shrug.

'Cat got your tongue?'

We are into the realm of banter now, and that I can cope with. It is after all why I have come. Jack's potatoes are no tastier than anyone else's, but what folk queue up for is the quality of his banter. So to get the ball rolling I ask, 'How's Len?'

Len, Jack's brother, is a well-known local builder and was my nextdoor neighbour when I lived in the other house.

Jack lobs back with, 'Len? You know Len. Up to this and that, making a fortune as usual.'

Not having seen each another for a couple of weeks, a range of possible topics for congenial banter opens up between us. Jack, though a Cockney, is of Irish extraction. Possible topics to crack up over range from the whisky-fuelled punches at a recent family wedding to the ultimate choice of a hat for Jack's wife's at the selfsame occasion. But fate is not with us. Suddenly, from nowhere, a woman with a shopping bag appears. She is not one of Jack's regulars and I doubt he has ever seen her before. But though banter with regulars is all well and good, business is business and Jack now turns his attention to her.

'Yes, Madam, what can I get you?'

I head now for Sally's stall. When it comes to the ups and downs of life, there is nothing like another woman. For a start we share the problems common to our gender. But, as fate would have it, Sally has a customer and is deep in negotiation. As with Jack, business comes first. Besides, now that I think of it, Sally and I will likely as not end up in tears. Suddenly, I begin to wonder what I am doing here. After all, I am not likely to be cooking many meals in the foreseeable, so there is no point in buying food. A passing woman glances at me sideways. Decides I look harmless and goes on her way. But it remains a fact that I am doing no good to anyone by standing here looking spare. I decide to return to the cats and my own four walls.

Letting myself in through the front door, I can hear the phone ringing in the kitchen, and who should it be but Anthea Goldsmith. This bucks me up no end. I seem to have been in purdah from normal life.

'How are you doing?'

'So-so.'

'I was wondering if you'd like to come to supper?'

I could not get the words out fast enough. Normality and the company of friends? No contest.

'Oh, I'd love to.'

'Good. Tomorrow?'

'Please. Oh yes, please.'

'We'll eat early. Shall we say six? John's working at home.'

There is a moment when I wonder if I should ask about Robin but then decide not to. It is enough to get out of the house and away from my ghosts.

As I replace the receiver I sense a hand on my back. When Ben wanted to show affection, he would often pat me like a dog. Warm and compassionate, Ben, who despised sentimentality, had a phrase for dealing with anything untoward and this had always been a brisk 'Get on with the next thing.' Older than Methuselah, Ben was a wise soul, from the moment he was born.

Next day Anthea greets me at the door with, 'I've a surprise for you.'

'Is it Robin?' I ask. Ever since we had spoken, the day after Ben was lost, I had frequently thought of talking to Robin. As I go in, John, who is busy talking to a man with a mop of unruly ginger hair, turns round to say, 'Shirley meet Robin – Robin, Shirley.'

That day when I spoke to Mark Litchfield's partner is crystal clear in my mind. *Marques*'s owner did not trouble himself to inform me of my son's death. He had left me to hear the news over the radio. Words can never express how I still feel about this. But later that morning, Robin, whom I had never met, phoned to offer me comfort. I would never forget that, so to meet him in the flesh is a big moment for me. There seemed no need for pleasantries and we went straight into a hug. Words are sometimes superfluous, and I felt that I already knew him.

Anthea chips in, 'You two get acquainted now while I finish getting the supper ready. Robin's driven all the way from Cornwall to meet you and he is starving.'

I turn to Robin. 'At last I can thank you.'

'For what?'

'Being a rock that day.'

Robin gives me a pat, which reminds me of Ben and this makes me want to cry. Then John asks Robin, 'Is it true that Mark tried to prevent you from having Shirley's number?'

Robin nods and there is silence as we take this in. Then Robin looks me in the eye and says, 'It was a truly remarkable feat, the way Ben got himself to the Caribbean under his own steam.'

'Not much fun for his mum,' remarks Anthea from the stove.

'I could not have stopped him even if I'd wanted to.'

'Is it true that he raised the cash to get himself out to the Caribbean by doing a window-cleaning round?'

That really makes me laugh. 'If you had known Ben, the very idea of someone paying him to clean anything is completely hysterical, but yes, it's true.'

There is a long pause and then I say, 'Having to hear about it in a news bulletin was...' but then find that I cannot go on.

John asks, 'Did Mark not send you a cable?'

'Not even a postcard.'

A chill falls over the room as everyone takes this in. But you cannot re-write the past and I have already begun to move on.

We settle down to eating and drinking and they begin talking about boats. Robin tells me about how he and John sailed to Tierra del Fuego on *Marques*.

'This was when the BBC filmed *The Voyage of Charles Darwin*.'

'A friend of mine spent two years filming a TV series on her.'

'You wouldn't be talking about Iain Cuthbertson, by any chance?'

'Yes. Why, do you know him?'

'Everyone knows Iain.'

I tell them Iain and I first met in Glasgow when rehearsing a TV series. At the time Ben had been a babe in arms. Much later, it was Iain who had given Ben the money for his first dinghy.

'Good heavens,' says John. 'There's a turn-up for the books.'

To change the subject I say, 'Can I ask you something, Robin? I know there was a dispute over ownership but at the time that *Marques* foundered, was she your boat...or Litchfield's?'

John looks at Robin, who sighs and says, 'We're still in dispute.'

Then I remembered seeing a newspaper photo of Robin, looking distraught. He had looked as if he was trying to hide from the camera. The caption said he had put spanners in *Marques*'s engine to prevent her from leaving. Robin knew then there was an issue with the vessel and that she was not safe.

My evening at John's has given me much to think about and I leave with more questions than answers. Then by some strange coincidence – having not seen Iain for over a year – he turns up on my doorstep a few days later. True to form he does not trouble to phone first. But that was hardly anything new. The bell rings and when I go to the door, Iain is standing on the step looking impatient. Exactly as if we had arranged a meeting or seen each other yesterday. At six foot four he looms up like a giant. Clearly this is not a social visit. We go straight into the sitting room, where Iain lowers himself onto the sofa, puts his head back and looks up at me unsmiling

'I had to come, darling...' he says, '...it's been on my mind since I heard. I watched that vessel be made more and more unsafe. She was a cargo vessel and top-heavy, a film prop, and she should never have been out in those seas.'

Iain had played Captain Kirkwood in *The Onedin Line* and filmed on *Marques* over a two-year period. A sailor in real life, he had a boat of his own. If anyone knew that ship he did, so I wait, knowing there is more to come.

'When we were filming it was always in daylight and we had a "rescue vessel" on hand. God knows why they let her enter that race.'

After that we sit in silence for a while but I know Iain has not finished. 'She was a film prop and that ridiculous poop deck they tacked on to make her more photogenic made her even more unstable.'

It is time to make my own confession. 'Did you know Ben sailed her in Spain at fourteen?'

'How did that come about?'

'I saw an ad for "an adventure holiday" in the *Sunday Times* for kids going out to Spain on a bus. It sounded like Ben's "thing". I should have asked questions then.'

Iain sighs. 'I wish you'd talked to me first.'

'Oh, Iain…' I say, '…you weren't even around. Besides, you know perfectly well that Ben always did his own thing. I was just his bloody mother.'

'Hindsight,' Iain mutters and shakes his head. He is clearly troubled. I don't see him for a long while afterwards. But that is par for the course.

There is someone else I have to see and that is Charlie Lanyon. Charlie had been First Mate at the time Ben joined *Marques*. In fact, it was he in person who had decided to take Ben on. Later he left, as did many others, all angry at Litchfield's slack leadership and disregard for safety. Back in the UK, Charlie rings, saying he would like to come and see me. I say to come anytime. On the phone he sounds anxious.

Once the house was full of young men; now it's just me and the cats. A day or so later, when the doorbell rings, Violet, Ben's cat, swishes past, like a bad-tempered woman in a ballgown. She cannot understand why Ben has not come back.

'Mrs Bryant?'

He looks young for a First Mate and I realize this must be an ordeal. Charlie is six foot tall with hair bleached by the sun, as Ben's was in the photos. Older and taller than Ben, they seem, in this moment, curiously alike. Also he wears a red Helly Hansen storm-coat exactly like the one I had bought Ben. It could almost be him standing there.

Charlie says again, 'Mrs Bryant?' and I realize I am staring at him.

'Charlie! What must you think of me, keeping you standing on the step like that. It was just…for a moment…'

Charlie says, 'It's fine, I understand,' and follows me into the kitchen.

'Tea or something stronger?' I ask.

Charlie laughs. 'What, in the middle of the afternoon? Tea will be fine, thanks.'

I put the kettle on and try to make conversation, as I can see he is nervous.

'When did you get back?'

'The day before yesterday.' He takes a breath, then says my name again. 'Mrs Bryant…'

'Shirley, please.'

'It took all my courage to ring you this morning.'

'Charlie,' I say softly, 'I do know it has been a shock for you too.'

Something passes over his face which I can't read and the air is heavy with the things we are not saying.

'I feel responsible…' he finally says.

'But you were not even on the boat.'

'No, but I was the one who took Ben on.'

'And he was thrilled; he had such an awful time racketing about in Antigua. Did you know he had to helm across the Atlantic without an automatic pilot?'

'Yes. He told me that day I met him on the quayside. Ben had guts and you can be very proud of him. Not many kids of eighteen could have coped. I was furious when I heard about that French guy making him tramp to customs and do all the stuff he should have been doing.'

'It must have been such a relief for him when he bumped into you. He wrote about it. You can imagine how pleased we were.'

'He had come on so much since I last saw him, really grown up.'

Tears spring to my eyes but this is an ordeal for him too and I must not make it worse.

'Charlie, no matter what happened that night, there is no way you were responsible; you were not even there!'

'No,' he says grimly, 'but I should have been. Litchfield was screwing everyone, which was why I left, but I had responsibilities. Ben was becoming a first-class sailor; he'd matured…' He brushes a hand across his eyes. 'You will never know how sorry I am. If I could do it again I would…'

'You must not think like that. There is no way you could possibly have anticipated what happened.'

'Maybe, but I will carry the guilt for the rest of my life.'

'How do you think Ben would feel if he could hear you? Listen to me, Charlie, I appreciate all you've said about Ben; it means a lot but you know yourself what Ben would have said: 'Get on with the next thing.' So let us talk about other things. I loved that story John Hamilton told us about you telling Ben to take some people ashore in the

Dory and him rushing off before you could finish what you were saying.'

But Charlie will not be diverted. 'It would not have happened if I had been there.'

'How can you say that? They are saying it was a storm.'

'A wooden boat does not overturn and sink to the bottom of the ocean because of a bit of weather.'

'I am guessing you did not get on with Mark Litchfield?'

Charlie knows he must watch what he says. There are legal implications. The crew had already been threatened and told to 'toe the party line'. I can still sense the anger.

He says, 'Latterly, no, which is largely why I left, but had I known…'

'Charlie, you were not even there, and in your shoes Ben would have done exactly as you did and left. Whoever is to blame here, it most certainly isn't you.'

7

THINGS START TO HAPPEN
SUMMER 1984

During Ben's six months away at sea I had grown used to seeing letters with foreign stamps lying on the mat. But now I begin to dread the post. A posthumous letter from Ben would be more than I could bear. Yet part of me longs to see his handwriting again.

One day a letter with a foreign stamp lies on the mat. I stand looking at it, scarcely daring to breathe. It was only when I picked it up that I saw, with a mix of relief and disappointment, it was not addressed in Ben's trademark scrawl but was typed and looked rather official. I went into the kitchen and sat on Ben's stool to read it. That stool was something I had picked up in a street market in Camden Town. Made of old pine it was probably crafted in the last century. During one of his DIY fits, Ben had used it as a sawboy and left a deep cut in the top. I had been furious at the time. Now it would forever remind me of him and had become precious. I had some instinct the letter must have to do with the disaster. As I slit it open with a knife, my heart was beating so fast that it took me a moment to take in. It was from a firm of New England lawyers, Lovett, Schefrin and Gallogly Ltd. Down the left-hand side was an impressive-looking list of lawyers' names. I glanced at the signature, Karen Davidson, in a typically American hand, and suddenly my mouth felt dry. I reached over to the sink to fill a mug with water, which I drank slowly. I guessed I was about to learn something about the disaster that killed Ben and so I braced myself.

But it turned out that what Karen Davidson wanted was to ask for information, not impart it. Having never set eyes on *Marques*, I was unable to help. She was seeking contact with lawyers in the UK acting for victims over here. But no one here, except me, had shown any interest. I went upstairs to type a reply. I had no information to offer but had said any she could give me would be very welcome. I gave her my telephone number. Then, looking at my watch, I saw the time and remembered I was meeting Peter in the pub. I wanted to discuss the Sailing Trust that I announced over the radio in that first flush of bereavement. I had spoken off the top of my head with no idea of how to set about it. Time to honour my promise.

Peter came back from the bar with his pint and my gin and tonic.

'Guess what,' I said, 'I've had a letter from America.'

'Is it to do with Ben?'

'Indirectly. It was from some lawyers in New England.'

'Typical.'

'What do you mean?'

'Money. It's the first thing the Americans think of. Have nothing to do with them.'

'Peter, you don't know that.'

He nodded. 'Oh yes, I do. What did they want?'

'Contact details of anyone over here who might be suing.'

'I rest my case.'

'Don't you want to know what happened?'

'I do know. Ben was killed.'

'But it's not that simple, is it? Don't you want to know more about how or why it happened?'

'No, because it won't bring him back. Nothing will now. I thought you said you wanted to talk about the Trust?'

'I do but I felt sure that you'd want to know about this letter.'

He shook his head. 'Do the Trust, love, do that for Ben.'

Then I remembered I had brought something to show him. 'I found this among Ben's papers...' and I thrust a sheet of paper under his nose. 'It seems Ben was ahead of us and already had a plan to teach disadvantaged kids sailing.'

As Peter fumbled for his glasses I said, 'Sit tight and I'll read it to you.'

'There can be no doubt that society's mistakes are the duty of society to correct. Not only is it morally wrong to punish the young person who has put his first foot forward in a way unacceptable to society, it is also counter-productive. An alternative is to help him before it is too late. I have experienced life on an old barquentine run by a German charity as an alternative to borstal. It is a simple lifestyle and a hard, sometimes uncomfortable life. Its values are simplicity and the freedom of the wind. The law is upheld to the minimum. They just sail and maintain their ship. Life is simple and easy. Everybody takes responsibility for housework, helming, lookout and sail changes. It is assumed people will take up their own responsibilities but there is no discipline. Ben Bryant.'

'Did you know he'd written this?' Peter asked.

'Don't be silly, it would have been more than my life was worth to go rooting around in his stuff. Ben guarded his privacy. I just thought you'd be interested.'

'I am. Listen, if you are thinking of setting up a Charitable Trust, why not call in at the library on your way home? They've got a good reference section. There's sure to be information on how to start.'

Then we went our separate ways. Peter had a meeting in town and I headed for the branch library at Southend Green where Ben used to do his newspaper round.

I decided to walk back over the Heath. It would be my first time there since that terrible day. Time to brave the memories. That was where Ben had made mud pies. Higher up the hill was his very own 'climbing tree'. I found myself remembering the day he came down Parliament Hill on his bike at speed and took a head bang. After he screamed that he could not see, I drove him straight to

Great Ormond Street Children's Hospital, terrified that he had lost his sight. He screamed blue murder but Sister suggested I go home and come back in the morning. Ben had a wail like a banshee. I could see that Sister had him down for a troublemaker. At 6 a.m. she rang to say that his sight had returned and he was rational. I arrived to find Ben surrounded by junior doctors and complaining bitterly that they were monopolizing his Tintin books.

But now as I'm standing here on the Heath, I realize that the answer to launching the Trust would be through publicity and I had an idea. A spot on *Woman's Hour* would be just the thing. I had contacts there, I knew Jenni Murray and had sometimes read the Book of the Week. Back home, I rang the *Woman's Hour* office. A secretary answered and said everyone had left but if I would care to outline the project, she would pass it on.

That night I went to bed early and was sound asleep when I was woken by the phone ringing in my study next door. I staggered in and picked up.

'Yes, hullo?' My heart was in my mouth. What now?

'Am I speaking to Shirley?'

'Yes. Please, who is this?'

'My name is Karen Davidson. I am a US attorney. You sent me your phone number.'

'But it is three o'clock in the morning!'

'Is it? Oh, I am so sorry. I must have been thinking New York time. But I felt sure you'd want to hear this; I have some news on *Marques*.'

My heart almost stopped.

'It would appear – my source is impeccable by the way – that *Marques* left illegally. She was never officially signed off.'

'What does that mean?'

'It means that she was never inspected.'

I was still in a fog. 'Are you saying this could have something to do with the disaster?'

'Very much so, I'm afraid. Did you know that your Prime Minister and the Minister for Transport were both involved?'

It was three o'clock in the morning and she was talking politics at me. I wondered what this could have to do with the disaster.

'It now appears likely that the boat was not seaworthy.'

'What?'

'Sail training vessels, or indeed any vessels carrying passengers or young trainees, must have an out-of-the-water examination. We know for certain this never took place. But your government are refusing to answer letters or take our calls.'

'Are you serious?'

'This could mean million-dollar lawsuits.'

I was thinking, more to the point, it might have led to Ben's death.

'How do you know all this?'

'Because we have Freedom of Information in the US. Shirley, it would appear that your Prime Minister, Margaret Thatcher, colluded.'

Wide awake now, I said, 'You can't possibly know that!'

'You have my word; that it is cast iron. Someone with more knowledge of your political system might know how this happened.'

Then she went over everything. It was the first time she had come across such a case. 'As for Mark Litchfield, he seems to be a man of some arrogance.' Then she went on, saying that there was nothing to be gained by contacting him but that they did urgently need to talk with the Department for Transport who, currently, were refusing to engage.

'My God, this all sounds so sinister!'

Karen agrees. 'That is why we need your help. As a British citizen you are entitled to ask questions and they will have to reply.' Meanwhile, she had decided to take a trip to Halifax, Nova Scotia to see what she could glean on the spot. In the first instance she suggested I should write to someone called Captain De Coverley at the Marine Division of the Department for Transport. She outlined the questions I should ask and said any information I could glean would be helpful and that she would be in touch when she got back from Halifax.

It was the end of sleep for that night. I was having trouble taking it all in. But with a sense of dread I knew it must be the truth. Who could I go to? Where to start? I must be careful. As for *Woman's Hour*, that would have to go by the board now. I lay awake wondering who to go to for advice. I knew to my cost that you can do more harm than good by rushing in too hastily.

THINGS START TO HAPPEN

I needed time to think. Get out of the house, I thought. Give yourself some space. I knew people in the media, but who would be the right one to approach? I must be careful and look before I leap. Take a break, I thought. There was no local market that day but there was one in Camden Town. It had been ages since I had been there. Reg, a Cockney, one of a vanishing breed, brought a handcart to Camden Market every week, with everything priced in old money – Reg scorned decimalization. A woman I knew had cleaned up by bulk buying his Victorian jugs and selling them on at Sotheby's. Then there were the food shops where you could buy olive oil. They had never heard of it, down Queen's Crescent. My policy has always been that after a sleepless night, ignore it and make up the sleep the following night. I was at the front door when the phone rang and had half a mind to ignore it. But curiosity got the better of me so I picked up.

'Hello?'

'Hi, is that the British lady?'

Yet another American: this one sounded as if he was from the Bronx, his manner and accent a million miles from Karen Davidson and her East Coast drawl. But another lawyer being the last thing on my mind, I was brisk.

'Who wants her?'

'Gee-whiz,' he said, 'you don't sound very British. Have I got the right dame?'

'That rather depends which dame you are after.'

'Straight from the shoulder,' he laughs. 'I like it. Would this be Shirley by any chance?'

For some reason his voice cheered me. So I said, 'Sure is,' making a stab at the accent. I had never been to America but had been an actor. This man did not sound like any lawyer I had ever met and I was curious.

'Wow, kid! Would you be one of those individuals bereaved on that darn boat?'

I answered soberly. 'Yes, my 18-year-old son was killed. Did you lose someone?'

'Hell no…' He fell over himself to apologize. 'Ma'am, I offer you my most sincere condolences. Doug Skinner, attorney, speaking. For sure I did not mean to disrespect you. I guess you already know we are taking a class action over here.'

'I don't know anything. I've had one call from a lawyer in Maine but as yet have not had the chance to check out what she told me.'

'Maine? A lawyer? Hey, would you be able to give me her name?'

'Sure,' and I gave him Karen's details. He thanked me profusely and ended the call saying, 'Now, you take care.'

I was out of the door before anyone else could ring, wondering if I would ever hear from Doug again. I rather liked the sound of him.

I pointed my red Mini in the direction of Camden Town and made a shopping list in my head as I drove. Olive oil. Maybe some nice fat black olives? I would go first to the Greek shop and then give Reg's barrow the once over. All the time, with last night's conversation running through my head, I decided to reserve judgement on what Karen had told me until I could find some way to check it out. This was clearly a political story, so best not to go round shouting the odds. Getting away from Grafton Road was a good idea and my head was already feeling clearer. I parked near the Roundhouse and headed for the market. The barrows were a feast for the eye. Why do UK supermarkets squash everything into layers of plastic? The French never do. I was admiring a glossy pile of aubergines, when I heard someone behind me say 'Shirley!' Turning I found myself face to face with Joan Bakewell.

Back in the days when we both worked in BBC radio and were also both married to men in the Drama Department, we had been on dinner-party terms. Now, Joan was divorced, as I was, and had a son of similar age to Ben, who was yet another sailing freak.

'I've been meaning to ring, you've been on my mind. How are you?'

'Not exactly sure, to be honest.'

'Oh, Shirley, it is bound to take time.'

'The worrying thing is the picture keeps changing.'

'In what way?'

'As you probably know, we were given to understand it was an accident.'

'And are you saying it wasn't?'

'It's not me saying. I've never set eyes on the boat. It's the Americans.'

'What Americans?'

'Lawyers for other victims. I had a phone call last night, in the small hours.'

'Did they forget the time difference?'

'God knows. I think she was too het up to care. They seem to know what happened but apparently our government is refusing to engage.'

'About what? Tell me more.'

'Not sure but it does sound fishy. Honestly, it's a miracle bumping into you.'

Joan looks at her watch. 'Let's go somewhere we can talk. Let's make it an early lunch and go to the new Chinese place, my treat.'

Over lunch, our conversation continues. 'This American lawyer,' Joan asks, 'did she sound as if she knew what she was talking about? Or was she just some nut?'

'She did sound deadly earnest and I've been racking my brains about who to talk to. You know what goes on behind government doors. I only came out to clear my head. It is serendipity bumping into you like this.'

'Try to remember what she said.'

'It's a bit of a jumble. It was the middle of the night. But I do remember her saying there was some inspection the boat should have had, which was skipped. It's coming back to me. She said that *Marques* had never had a proper inspection. I think she called it an Exemption Certificate.'

'That can't be right. It's a negative.'

'Or was it some kind of load...? Lorry load, would that be it?'

'Did she say Load Line Exemption Certificate?'

'How clever of you to know.'

'It's my job to be a mine of largely useless information. That's for boats outside the normal criteria. Boats like *Marques* in fact, so you've probably got that right. The law says they must have an out-of-the-water examination to make sure they are stable and seaworthy. Does she claim that they skipped it? We should be cautious here, as it would be a serious offence.'

'One thing I do remember was that she said it was all down to lack of Freedom of Information in the UK.'

'Yes, it's obligatory in the States, as it should be here. We'll catch up eventually.'

'I should have taken notes but was only half awake'

'Any vessel leaving British shores with paying passengers must have an official survey, just as a car has to have an MOT. There's no getting around that. That's what I can't understand. You might get some rogue owner trying to dodge regulations but not a government department. It's their job to keep us safe. That's what we pay them for. Keep this under your hat for now as it could be a very hot potato indeed.'

8

TAKING ACTION
1984

Next morning, I had trouble believing yesterday ever happened.

Before all hell broke loose, I had been playing around with an idea for a radio play but procrastination runs in a writer's blood. So I climbed out of the bathroom window and began to deadhead the geraniums. I was in the act of climbing back in when I heard the phone ring in my study and thinking it might be Joan Bakewell, hurried to answer.

'That was quick!'

'Is that Miss Cooklin?'

'Sorry, who is this?'

'BBC *Woman's Hour*. You spoke to one of our researchers.'

'Yes.'

'Could you outline the idea for me?'

'My son was killed in the *Marques* disaster. I want to found a Charitable Trust in his memory. Sailing for inner-city kids. I thought it might make an item for *Woman's Hour*.'

'Sounds interesting. It's short notice, I know, Miss Cooklin, but would you be free tomorrow?'

'Yikes!'

'You're not free?'

'Yes, no, I mean…sorry, you took me by surprise.'

'We've got a bit of a situation here. Tomorrow's guest has been taken ill. We wondered if you might be free?'

I said I was, but when I put the phone down I began to panic. Then I got out Ben's letters and started looking through them, with one ear tuned in case Joan rang. I needed an idea. I thought of Bobby that day at Heathrow Airport and tried to centre on that.

Next day I set out early and parked in Portland Place, right opposite Broadcasting House, muttering my mantra: 'Lucky in parking meters, unlucky in love'. It usually works. Then I hurried through those great bronze doors, got in the lift and pressed the button for the second floor.

After we had exchanged pleasantries, Jenni Murray said, 'Let's make this informal, shall we? I'll prompt and you tell us about Ben and his journey in your own words. How does that sound?'

All of a sudden I felt the nerves kick in. It can happen to anyone. Jenni noticed and said, 'Perhaps you might start with why you decided on a Sailing Trust? Listeners might be surprised, in view of the way Ben was killed.' I said, 'It was something he had planned to do himself one day, so it's a way of following his wishes.' Jenni said that seemed a good place to start, then the red light blinked and we were on air.

'Tell us how you felt when Ben told you he was taking off for the Caribbean.'

'I knew arguing was useless. Ben was pig-headed. Once he had made up his mind it was hard to shift him.'

'Like most teenagers. Is it true he raised the cash by cleaning windows?'

That made me smile. The idea of Ben cleaning anything was funny. His domestic skills were confined to putting crockery on top of the dishwasher. She asked where his talents did lie. I said he had the gift of the gab and she replied, 'Oh, so another writer in the making.'

That set me off. I found myself talking about the Rabbi and how he said Ben was 'not a great window cleaner but a great talker'. I said I'd brought some of his letters and would like to read them aloud. My nerves had gone by now and the words flowed. In no time at all the red light was winking again and Jenni was saying, 'Thank you, Shirley, for telling us your story. You have been through every parent's worst nightmare. A Trust to encourage young people to find adventure will make a lasting tribute to Ben. Come back when the Trust is a working concern and tell us about it.'

As we came off air, Jenni said, 'Well done. I think that went really well. We're going over the road for some plonk. Will you join us?'

Once across the road and in the bar, I was soon part of a group. Betty Davies was there, in one of her big hats, and Archie Campbell was looking harassed. I was back in my element. Yet in the back of my mind I was wondering what progress Joan Bakewell was making and drove home slowly, conscious of the alcohol in my bloodstream, to park right outside my own front door. As I slammed the car door and hurried to put the key in my lock, my mind was on strong black coffee. But once through the front door, I found myself crunching on broken glass. Having never had a break-in, I did not know what to do first. Find a broom and sweep it all up or ring the police? I listened in case anyone was still in the house. Then I realized they had broken a side window, halfway up the stairs. The lock had held so they had not effected an entry. The house was silent, empty. I sidestepped the broken glass to get a dustpan. The window they tried to break in through was inaccessible from the outside, unless you had a ladder. What did they call people who entered houses that way? Cat burglars. My two cats were mewing piteously. I had a quick snivel and decided to ring the police. It had been an attempted break-in. Were you supposed to report those? A leaflet from the police had recently dropped through the door and was still on the dresser. I perused it. 'If you need advice on security, ring this number,' so I rang. The officer I spoke to said a constable was not far away and he would ask him to call in. The cats had begun to calm down when there was a ring at the door.

A fresh-faced young man stood on my doorstep. Pinned down to describe him I would have said he looked like someone on his way back from rugby practice.

'Mrs Cooklin?'

'It's not Mrs and please call me Shirley. What's your name?'

'Simon. You've requested advice on keeping your home secure.' He took off his helmet, parked it on the kitchen table and looked round. 'I gather you've had a break-in?'

'Well, they tried to get in, and I came home to find broken glass, but they didn't succeed. It says on your leaflet that police will advise on security.'

'So, nothing's been taken?'

'No. Apparently the lock held.'

He glanced up at the broken window. 'You've been lucky. Break-ins are a common occurrence round here.'

I stood up for Kentish Town. 'I prefer this area to Hampstead.'

'We have a lot of high-rise blocks in this area. They breed troublemakers. Shall we take a look round and check your locks? I may be able to advise on improving your security. But well done for keeping that side window locked. Most people don't bother.'

'I wouldn't have thought a house like this was worth breaking into.'

'Kids,' he says

'Why do they do it?'

'Boredom. Kids in high-rise flats with nothing better to do.'

I thought of Ben doing his paper round and buying his 'sounds' with his own money and said, 'Not all kids.'

'No, but we get more than our share round here'

We toured the house together. Once he had 'cased' all the openings I offered to make him a cup of coffee. He was clearly new at the job and seemed too educated to be a humble beat officer. Making a guess I cheekily asked what he read at university. He said, 'No thanks' to the coffee and to the second question replied, 'Modern History.'

I wondered aloud why a young man with a degree would choose to be a copper.

'Why not,' he said, 'it's a career. The Met is a huge organization. There's something for everyone.'

'If you say so.'

'About this break-in, I could probably collar the little lot who did this, but they'd only get a caution and be back at it the next day. It seems a pointless exercise and a waste of public money.'

'So what's the answer?'

'There isn't one.'

I thought aloud. 'Maybe there is.'

Simon changed his mind about the coffee and we sat down to chat. He had guessed the young man in the *Ham & High*, who died in a sailing disaster, was my son and asked if he was right. I said he was and we talked about Ben. I told him about the window cleaning and the Rabbi, but mostly I talked about boats and Ben's passion to sail to the other side of the world. I told him too of my own experience of learning to sail at seventeen and how, as a young person, I found something I needed in the freedom of the sea. I said I wanted something positive to come out of the tragedy and that my son would have wanted that too. I told him I had just come from doing a broadcast to publicize the idea. The Trust was a pipe dream but I hoped to turn it into a reality. From what he had said it seemed there was a need for an antidote to inner-city boredom.

Simon's eyes lit up. 'I think it's a fantastic idea. When are you going to get started?'

I said, 'It's all very well to have a bright idea but we're nowhere near the sea here.'

'True. Not many boating lakes in Camden but what about the Welsh Harp in Wembley? I know for a fact that they have sailing there.'

We spent over an hour talking. Then Simon looked at his watch and said his sergeant would think he had been kidnapped and he'd best get back to the station. We had already agreed to take a trip to the Welsh Harp one Sunday soon and do a recce. At last I could see a way forward to making the Trust a reality. Simon was exactly what I needed – a partner to help me get the Ben Bryant Trust off the ground.

But as far as the *Marques* mystery was concerned, knowing the full story seemed as far away as ever.

9

THE PLOT THICKENS
LONDON, 1984

Joan rang the next day. She said everything had checked out and the main issue was that something illegal had definitely taken place, and whatever her reasons, the Prime Minister had decided to face it out, rather than take the legal route. One should bear in mind that we were up against a very tough cookie.

'Where does that leave us?'

'I am not too sure. The story is dynamite. It's hardly surprising Thatcher was cagey. It seem no one less than a government minister was behind this.'

'So, she was right then, this US lawyer?'

'Apparently. Our friend Mark Litchfield has friends in very high places.'

'I thought we already knew that.'

'It's the scale of it that gets me. Apparently, he got his MP, Andrew Rowe, to take his request to the junior

minister and made it sound harmless, but he was breaking the bloody law when his job is to uphold it. I mean,
if some chap in a garage did that, they'd throw the book
at him.'

'When it got as far as the minister, why didn't he put a
stop to it?

'It seems to have got a bit *Boys' Own*. [Nicholas] Ridley
[the Minister for Transport] called in his surveyors and
suggested they take the so-called 'independent surveyor'
out for a pint.'

'What had a "pint" got to do with it?'

'To see if he was "one of the boys". Have you ever heard
such blokeish rubbish? They made him sign a bit of paper,
accepting responsibility. It was a farce. The guy doesn't
have a penny to his name. When *Marques* foundered, there
were very red faces in Whitehall, but Thatcher will not let
this stick to Ridley.'

'Joan, we're not talking about a parking infringement.
Nineteen people died.'

'I thought you'd want to know what you're up against.'

'Do the press know?'

'They know something fishy went on. But Thatcher
won't sacrifice Ridley. They're thick as thieves those two.
He's part of her plan for Britain.'

'So?'

'She'll kick it into the long grass or call an internal
inquiry. That's the government's last line of defence when
they want to take the heat off. No statements can be issued

and they can keep it up as long as they like. You could be talking next year, or even the one after.'

'Which leaves us where exactly?'

Joan cogitated. 'Hmm…we might consider it for *Newsnight*.'

'Would you, really?'

She looked enigmatic. 'I've got a keen young producer, Nicola Shearer; it's right up her street.' Then she said she would get on to her but also gave me her phone number and I was so excited I couldn't wait.

A voice came on the line. 'Nicola Shearer's phone.'

'Hello, I'm a friend of Joan Bakewell's and she's going to ring you, but I couldn't wait, so…'

'Oh, hi. Shirley? Yes, Joan gave me your number and I was intending to call you later.'

'Is this a bad moment?'

'Not at all. Would you like to meet today?'

'If you are free.'

'I've been looking at the clippings on the *Marques* disaster and I'm keen to get going. Am I right that you live in Kentish Town?'

'Yes.'

'Then I'll come to you, if that suits. Shall we say, eleven tomorrow?'

The very next day we faced each other across the kitchen table. Nicola pushed her coffee cup away along with the newspaper clippings. 'Joan says you are a writer. If you were researching this, where would you start?'

I thought about this. 'Two people stand out in my memory. The first is Robin Cecil-Wright, Litchfield's erstwhile partner, the second is a man called Colin Searle.'

She opened her notebook. 'Who is he?'

'He's Race Director for the Sail Training Organization, who were in charge of the race. He's a volunteer but Colin struck me as being efficient. I was in a hell of a state and he seemed to understand what I was going through. The search went on for almost a week. There was an air–sea rescue and other boats in the vicinity. Then he rang me to say the search was being called off. I sat there like an idiot waiting for him to tell me what would happen next. But he just said, "We are winding down." I said, "Surely that can't be it. There must be something more. For instance, I would like to meet Ben's friends, the survivors." I think he was taken aback but he decided it was a good idea and said he would get back to me.'

'Did he?'

'Yes. He arranged a private meeting at Heathrow Airport, for survivors and relatives of the three British victims. It was to be held beyond customs, well away from roving reporters.'

'That sounds both imaginative and compassionate.'

'It helped everyone. Bereaved and survivors alike. Bobby, Ben's best friend, walked in looking like a ghost. Andy, the sparks, who'd been alone in a lifeboat for twelve hours, was in shock. My selfish idea turned out to be good for everyone. We were able to laugh, cry and let off steam. I have a lot of time for Colin Seale. It was a day I will never forget.' As I said this, I sighed. It seemed now like something that had happened to someone else.

Nicola said, 'You have given me a real sense of the day. Not sure what to do about Robin and his injunction. But there's a way round most things if you look hard enough. I'll be in touch when I have something to report.'

That was the last I would see of Nicola for some months but we kept in touch by phone. Then she went to America to film for the programme, so was out of my life for a month or so. Then, in January, Doug phoned. Litchfield was trying to 'muzzle' anyone who had any connection with *Marques* and issuing injunctions like confetti. He said he was putting a copy in the post to me, of what he called 'this gagging order'.

A day or so later, Peter rang. He had seen Litchfield on TV saying that a public inquiry would be 'a waste of time and public money' and it made him feel sick. He'd changed his mind about doing something. I asked if he would come with me to see the MP, Frank Dobson. He said he would, work permitting.

In February, I decided it was time to write to De Coverley again. I reminded him nine months had passed since the 'internal inquiry' began. Nothing could justify such a delay. His reply came suspiciously fast, leading me to conclude that the report had been finished months ago.

This turned out to be right and they had been sitting on it. On all sides I was being told that next year was the earliest possible date and it was even whispered that the year after looked more likely. They were stalling. I had extracted a promise from my MP Frank Dobson that he would ask a Parliamentary Question and we would take it from there. He would be in touch once he heard anything.

It took three weeks for the Question to be answered, and then it was not by the Minister, Nicholas Ridley, but another minister. Clearly Ridley was trying to distance himself. Three more weeks went by. Six weeks after our meeting, Dobson telephoned saying he would put a copy of the Answer in the post, but for the record, he would read it out now over the phone: 'Matters of this kind will be considered at the Formal Investigation into the loss of *Marques*. For that reason, it would not be appropriate for me to comment in advance.'

So, that was it. We were gagged and bound and the government could stall as long as it liked. I pointed out that it was almost a year already. Dobson got on his high horse and started talking protocol. I much regretted the stepping down of Jock Stallard, my old MP, who would have handled it very differently.

I decided it was time for some 'freelancing'. Frank Dobson had made his feelings plain about such 'untidy' behaviour. Too bad, I thought, it's not your son who died. Then, one day, while out on the Heath, I caught sight of Michael Foot walking his dog and hurried to catch up. I reminded him that

Ben had been his paperboy and gave him an outline of the situation. He asked me to send a letter to his office. Then I decided to write to any MPs who might be interested. I racked my brains. Labour's Bill Rogers and his wife Sylvia were once neighbours. I wrote to him. Giles Radice's wife was a friend and our daughters were besties. I added Edward Heath's name on the grounds that he was a sailor. I included David Owen as I thought him a good egg and I wrote to the Leader of the Opposition, Neil Kinnock. That letter remained unanswered so I wrote again, protesting at the Labour Party's lack of interest. To be in no doubt this time, I enlisted the help of a friend who lived on the same road as the Kinnocks and pushed it through their letter box. All credit to Glenys Kinnock, who picked up the phone next day and rang to apologize. She said things sometimes slipped through the net. All the letters generated answers but with one vital exception: my letter to Nicholas Ridley, Minister for Transport and the man behind the tragedy. He was too grand to answer letters from the likes of me. The pile of paperwork on my desk grew but still nothing was happening.

As for Nicola Shearer, for some months we were not in touch and when she came back from the US she was mostly in Kent, interviewing Litchfield. Flattered the BBC were making a film about him, he sang like a canary. The valuable footage Nicola had obtained proved a double-edged sword as later he was able to sue her in court. So, it was not until May 1985 that she rang to apologize and asked if she could come to Grafton Road to film a clip of

Peter and me for the programme. While the crew were setting up lights, we finally caught up. I wanted to know if the leads I had given her proved useful. With Robin, there had been a problem because of the injunction. She said breezily they got over that by having him walk towards the camera, his mouth tightly closed, with presenter Robin Denselow at his side. As Robin remained mute, Denselow explained airily that Robin was barred from speaking because his erstwhile partner, Mark Litchfield, had taken out an injunction against him. This was clever because it made the injunction a talking point while giving the viewer a full-face view of a blameless-looking Robin.

I was working myself up into a fever. If the government was covering something up, something which seemed more certain every day, it was logical they should toe the party line. This did not make sense. It ought to be headline news. Let the public judge for themselves. I decided to ring the *Sunday Times*. Something else was going on here. Mark Litchfield was one thing, but he was only one man. Nicholas Ridley in the Department for Transport had done an old boy a favour by allowing a vessel without paper-work to sail. But the whole thing stank.

I looked up the phone number of the *Sunday Times* and asked for the Editor.

'He's not available,' said a voice on the line.

'Well, who can I speak to? This is urgent.'

He said he would put me through to the Deputy Editor. I asked his name.

'David Sinclair.'

By now, incoherent with rage and losing all sense of decorum, I yelled, 'Why aren't you speaking out?!'

'Who is this?'

'A great paper like the *Sunday Times*. It should be on the front page!'

'Who the blazes…'

I was beside myself. Frustration and anger had welled up in me and I screamed, 'I'm the mother of one of the young men killed in the *Marques* disaster! Why are you letting the government get away with this? A paper of your stature…'

'Your name, please,' he said firmly.

'What's my name got to do with it? They have committed a crime and you should be calling them to account.'

He asked for my name again and after I'd given it he said accusingly, 'You are a writer, aren't you?'

'I'm a scriptwriter.'

'You have written newspaper articles?'

'The odd one, yes.'

'And now you are telling me how to do my job. Well, that's just too bad as I hereby commission you to write it. Two thousand words, by the day after tomorrow,' and then he slammed the phone down.

I was in shock. I had asked for his help and he had thrown the ball back. I was in no state to write my own name, never mind an article. How could I have been so stupid? This needed a political journalist. Then the anger drained away and professionalism kicked in. He had given me a commission. Ours is not to reason why. Something Ben had said in that last-ever phone call came back to me. He had mentioned *Tai-Pan*. When, in all innocence, I asked what it was, he had jeered, 'Call yourself a writer?' He was right. I thought of that last phone call and picked up a pen and began to write.

Just over a year ago, the spirited young crew of a three-masted British barque named Marques *set sail from Puerto Rico for Bermuda, on the first leg of the Tall Ships Race, 1984. As sleeker and faster boats disappeared over the horizon, they abandoned hopes of winning and settled down to enjoy the sail. Yet when they blew into Bermuda harbour, they were greeted with shouts of 'You've won!'*

On June 2, 1984, with spirits high and all sails set for the benefit of the TV cameras, they crossed the line in Bermuda bound for Halifax, Nova Scotia, on the second leg of the race. At 2 am four of the crew were called out to go aloft and take down one of the sails. Afterwards they sat on the yardarm for a quiet smoke. Two of these young men were not to survive the night. One of them was my son Ben, aged just 18.

What exactly took place, a mere two hours later, is shrouded in mystery. There have been rumours of an adverse weather report, released too late, of a squall or a waterspout. Certainly, some violent freak of nature must have struck Marques *that night, but why a wooden boat that should have bobbed like a cork, sank to the bottom of the ocean in only 45 seconds, is far from clear. More disturbingly, since 19 lives were lost, a year later the mystery remains. What the parents and relatives of those lost on both sides of the Atlantic want to know, is why?*

In the first shock, Ben's father and sister and I had to learn to accept that an act of God had robbed us of Ben – adventurous and courageous Ben, whom we had not seen for nine months, not since he left school and first set sail for the Caribbean. Then it was announced that the Department for Transport, Marine Division, was to conduct a full investigation into the disaster. It would be painful but at least we would know the full story.

Months dragged by. Letters to the department requesting to know its findings only met with more letters, full of expressions of regret but short on information. Concern mounted, rumours abounded, we began to ask questions.

A request to see the marine survey of Marques, *prepared by John Perryman of Great Yarmouth, met with polite evasion. We learnt that while full insurance had been paid out for the boat, the crew were expected to take out their own medical insurance, in spite of the fact that they received only expenses in return for their services. The boat's owner, Mark Litchfield, obtained an injunction in the High Court to prevent his partner, Robin Cecil-Wright, from speaking about the affair to the Press and to parents of the dead or their representatives.*

Then recently, 10 months after the investigation began, questions were asked in Parliament. A Public Inquiry was speedily announced. I learn of this, not from the Transport Department, with whom I had exchanged so many letters, but from the media. From the same source I learnt with dismay that this inquiry was unlikely to begin until next year.

If the department has opted for a public inquiry after 10 months of investigation, then it must know something that I do not. I feel I have a right to know what it is. The dragging of feet, the evasion and the secrecy, which continue to surround the Marques tragedy are disturbing. It is hard to come to terms with the death of a child. To be uncertain whether or not that tragedy was the result of negligence is unbearable. The public inquiry will inevitably dredge up painful feelings for those who lost a child or relative. The hope of each one of us must be that the disaster will, in the end, be proved to have been, indeed, an act of God. Yet in the light of the past year's delays and evasions, conjectures about possible causes of the accident have accrued and there are those among us who have begun seriously to doubt that the event could not have been foreseen or prevented. If there is anything to reveal, revealed it must be. Certainly, the findings of the inquiry must be in the interests of all who put to sea. At no time is such concern more apposite than in International Youth Year. Tragic news events since the Marques disaster include a bomb in a Brighton hotel, a tiny girl beaten and killed by her stepfather, 53 people burned to death at one football stadium and 38 crushed to death at another. Concerned reaction to these events was swift and rightly so. A statement was made in the Commons two days after Bradford: the public inquiry began at once. Yet a full year after Marques went down we are no nearer to knowing the facts.

Ben was one of three Britons who died in Marques, young men to be proud of. Not for them the need to find excitement in anti-social behavior, or the depression of the dole queue. With others of Ben's family, I founded the Ben Bryant Trust in his memory, a charity to enable the disadvantaged young to learn to sail.

Adventure and risk are part of life: negligence that leads to death is shameful. Did Marques *founder through negligence? And if so, whose? For the sake of the sea-going young of today and tomorrow, it is high time that the mystery of* Marques *was revealed.*

It was late when I got to bed. Next day I rang the paper to say the article was ready and they said they would send a messenger, and did I have a head and shoulders of Ben? It was now in the lap of the gods.

Late that Saturday I went to King's Cross to buy a copy of the following day's *Sunday Times*. I opened the paper. The sub had not changed a word. I went back home and waited. Nothing happened. Monday passed, as did Tuesday and Wednesday. Still nothing. But what had I expected, some knight in shining armour to leap to my defence? Thank heaven there was still *Newsnight*.

On Thursday, needing to be on the move, I decided to drive to Swiss Cottage to do some shopping, or that was my intention, but the car wouldn't start. I went back inside and rang the AA. The skies had gone dark and it had started to drizzle. By the time the mechanic arrived it had become a downpour. Feeling guilty I took shelter while the poor man worked on in the rain. When the job was done I invited him in to dry-off and was in the act of filling the kettle to make him a cup of tea when the phone rang.

It was David Sinclair, Deputy Editor of the *Sunday Times*. I almost dropped the phone when he said, 'Shirley, great news! Two carpenters in Spain, who worked on the refit, have rung the paper. It looks like we've struck oil!'

'What do they say?'

'According to this guy Gavin, the hull was unseaworthy. They told Litchfield that she needed a proper overhaul, out of the water. He said he could not afford it and told them to patch her up but refused to authorize any major work, he said they should just do some caulking and nail a few planks. We've got him.'

I suddenly realized I had been hoping it would prove to have been an act of God. That Ben did not die because some unscrupulous man gambled with lives for the sake of a few lousy quid. David could hear I was falling apart. 'I did wonder if I should phone,' he said. 'But you must have known something like this was on the cards. After all, that was why you wrote that article. We've got evidence now to challenge the Department for Transport.'

He was right. What use was I, if I fell at the first hurdle? He said my reaction was natural but that we must be focused. He had assigned a reporter. With any luck, there would be a follow-up on the front-page next Sunday.

By the time I put the phone down I was ready to burst into tears. But I was not alone. The poor AA man, standing there soaking wet, had fallen headfirst into someone else's tragedy. Feeling I had little choice, I told him the whole story.

What would be the outcome? Two carpenters against Litchfield? I wanted to believe we had cracked it, but only time would tell.

10

ENTER THE NOBLE LORD
LONDON, JUNE 1985

On Saturday morning, on hearing the cats scrabble at my door, I realized I must have overslept. I pulled on a gown and started downstairs, both cats round my ankles trying to trip me up. I was halfway down when I heard something like a laugh. Ben was around early and up to his tricks. Then I saw a long envelope lying on the mat and my nose began to twitch, as if I were drinking champagne, and I heard again that faint laugh and wondered if it was coming from the street. I picked up the envelope. My name and address were written in a bold black hand. This was someone sure of their place in the world. Turning it over I saw the royal seal on the back and slit it open with a finger. Inside were several typed sheets and a letter in longhand, above which someone had typed 'From: The Lord Napier and Ettrick, 6 June 1985.'

Dear Miss Cooklin

I have read with not a little interest, and some very real sympathy, the article that you wrote for last Sunday's 'Sunday Times'.

I happened to be in Bermuda on official business at the time of the Tall Ships Race last year. I was staying with the Governor, Lord Dunrossil, and we visited several of the ships at anchor the day before the start of the second leg of the race. Included in these was Marques, we spent a good ten minutes talking with the Captain and members of the crew. I took photographs.

I watched the start of the race from the bridge of a Frigate of the Royal Canadian Navy in stormy conditions and watched the barque sail towards the north.

I have my own opinion as to what probably happened, but the story you tell in your article is, I believe, a dreadful reflection of what does happen after such a tragedy.

I shall be only too happy to do whatever I can to help you get a full investigation into the disaster. I would be pleased to meet you if you would like this. Negligence, if it were negligence, that leads to death is inexcusable, and such matters should not just be swept 'under the carpet'.

I have tabled a question for written answers in the House of Lords for a start.

Yours sincerely

Napier and Ettrick

As I stood there with the letter in my hand, I forgot to breathe for a moment, as I realized Lord Napier must have been one of the last people on earth to see my Ben alive. I thought of the laughter, which I had thought came from the street and decided Ben must have been up to his tricks. I went into the kitchen and picked up the telephone to dial Peter's number.

'Guess what?'

'Go on.'

'I've had a letter about my article...' I allowed myself to pause '...from a Lord!'

'A what?'

'No, not a "what", a "who"...a Member of the House of Lords. Do try to keep up, darling. He was on board *Marques*, only hours before she went down. He wants to help.'

'Good God'!

As I put the phone down, I remembered that day I took Ben to the House of Lords to see Frank Longford, a friend from my 'prison visiting' days. He had invited us to tea. Ben, astonished at being divested of his battered pilot's flying jacket by a flunky, began to question Frank about how you became a Lord. Frank, amused by this, had said, 'Well, first of all you must be very old' and Ben lost interest. Later, after Frank had treated us to tea and cakes in the restaurant, Ben had been amazed to see him take out a battered leather wallet to extract a couple of notes. He had been unable to understand why a Lord should be expected to pay. Surely he must get his cream cakes free, as a matter of course, or what was the point of being a Lord?'

I began to wonder if there was some connection, and as I stood there, in my nightie, puzzling, the phone rang.

'Hello.'

'Could I speak to Shirley Cooklin?' It was a nice voice, with an edge of humour.

'That's me, how can I help?'

'Mick Brown, *Sunday Times*, my editor gave me your number. I'm doing a piece for tomorrow's paper on *Marques* and I'm hoping you can help.'

'Hi Mick, what a coincidence, I was just about to call David. There's been a rather astonishing reaction to my article.'

He was instantly alert. 'Do tell.'

'I've had a letter from someone called Lord Napier.'

'Why is he writing to you? You do know who he is?'

'No.'

'He's the Private Secretary to one of the royals, Princess Margaret.'

'Good heavens. He says he was in Bermuda at the time of the race and went on board *Marques* with the Governor of Bermuda. That they both remarked on the state of the ship and that he has his own idea of what happened.'

'This is the most incredible piece of luck.'

'What's more, he's put his money where his mouth is and already tabled a question in the House of Lords. I'm about to write a reply, which I shall hand deliver to St James's Palace.'

'Wait till I tell David. He'll be dead chuffed. All thanks to your piece. Well done, by the way, we shall all have to look to our laurels.'

'You are too kind,' I said facetiously, 'but you rang me, how can I help?'

'I'm not interrupting anything?'

'Course not, anyway this takes precedence, fire away.'

And that was how it all began.

11

TWENTY DAYS
LONDON, 1985

After that, for the next twenty days, from the moment Lord Napier posed his 'Question' until the day we received the Prime Minister's response, it seemed as if everyone in London wanted to talk to me.

Sunday 17 June morning: I write a 'thank you' to Lord Napier, don blue boiler suit, and get ready to hand-deliver a reply to St James's Palace. My daughter smiles at my outfit. 'That's my mum,' she says and for once approves of me. I drive to Camden Town, heading for St James's Palace. I have just found a parking space when a duty policeman comes up to ask my business. I explain I want to hand-deliver a letter to Lord Napier and Ettrick. He gives me an old-fashioned look and says he will deliver it. Clearly, I am not to be trusted.

Sunday 17 June evening: I ring Lord Napier, as asked, thank him then say I want action. He says we must wait for the answer to his written question. I point out we have been waiting a year already. Yes, but all will flow from the written answer, he says. We exchange phone numbers. He will ring once he hears anything.

Monday 18 June: Edward Heath's Private Secretary rings, in answer to my letter asking for his help. On reflection, he cannot add anything to what I have already done.

Tuesday 19 June: Mick rings. An Alec Bilby insists on speaking to me. I say I will only do it sitting beside him. Mick thinks I'm a wimp. Call from Canadian TV producer, Catherine Outried, who wants an interview in July.

Wednesday 20 June: Mick reckons Bilby's genuine. That evening, Peter and I attend a Writers' Guild event at the Clarendon Hotel, Tottenham Court Road. Dinner afterwards with John Goldsmith. Peter challenges him to decide where his loyalties lie, says he must 'stand up and be counted'. John remarks that the reason for the delay is to protect Litchfield's insurance payout from Lloyd's.

Thursday 21 June: Busy day, mostly on the phone. Mick rings. The 'meet' with Bilby is put back to next week. Suspect I'm right and he is linked to Litchfield. I am well out of it. *Sunday Times* ring, Litchfield has issued a writ following Mick's piece. Not good news. Later Nicola says Litchfield has dropped his writ against BBC. Good news. This might give them the confidence to cover the story. Call Simon Winchester, as arranged, but find I'm speaking to his wife. He's been detained in Sri Lanka, for being where he ought not to have been. She expects him to be deported but he is currently in his hotel room sans passport. She does not expect him home before next week. I phone Lord Napier who has left for the day.

Friday 22 June morning: Lord Napier rings early. The answer to his question has arrived. 'This is for your ears only. An Inquiry was scheduled for January or February next year but thanks to my question it will now be October this year!' I can't thank him enough but he stops me saying, 'A way to go yet.'

Wednesday 26 June: Andrew Harvey, BBC, rings. With the injunction lifted he would like to do a story but the lawyers are wary. Can't tell him my news as not yet official. Depart lighthearted, for Jardin des Gourmets, Greek Street, lunch with Jane Ennis, *TV Times*. They are doing a piece on the Trust in July. Take taxi, as running late. Lunch till four.

Thursday 27 June morning: Letter from Thatcher's office. Not the letter but one from her Private Secretary acknowledging mine to Transport Secretary Ridley. Ring David Sinclair at home to check in. I say I'm furious about Ridley, the only one not to reply, and he's the one bloody responsible! David reckons best way to handle it is via letter to the Editor. Lord Napier's letter, plus mine and the one from MP Frank Dobson, are all useful for Litchfield's libel writ. Long talk with BBC lawyer Glen Del Medico who reckons Robin and Litchfield 'took BBC for a ride' in the filming of *Darwin*. Not too keen on John Goldsmith either, it seems.

Thursday 27 June afternoon: Long chat with Bill Anderson, Secretary of Sail Training Association, worried the tragedy will discourage parents from sending kids sailing. He talks of what he calls 'money-grabbing US lawyers' helping Antiguan families. 'I'll tell you what stinks,' I say, 'the "old boy" network which led to nineteen deaths.' Then add '...negligence will be found'. I speak to a French maritime consultant and later chat with Elizabeth Hamilton about safety at sea. Round day off with call from Catherine Outried who is keen to interview Lord Napier, so will I put a word in.

Saturday 29 June: Ron, Bobby's father, to stay, he has business in London. Keeps saying he wants truth to come out, but no one will put money where mouth is. We both worry Litchfield may pressurize Bobby.

Monday 1 July: *TV Times* to take photographs for Trust article. The cats get in on the act. Welcome publicity. Must soon start fund-raising in earnest.

Tuesday 2 July: About to go out as *Washington Post* ring. Talk for an hour. Give them Gavin's and Nicola's numbers. Piece to be in Thursday's paper. Then at last an answer from Ridley (or his Private Secretary). Inquiry to start October. Report back to Lord Napier, who says, 'That's progress.' Karen Davidson writes *Inca* has powderpost beetle. At 7.45 Alan Ravenscroft from 'Filmscreen Tonight' drops by and stays for supper. Wants to cooperate on *Marques* story. Catherine Outried rings, to say she's not yet spoken to Lord Napier.

Wednesday 3 July, 9 a.m.: I ring Lord Napier to say letter finally arrived from Secretary of State about Inquiry in October. He is delighted. Mention Canadian TV. He'll think about it, not yet seen *Newsnight*. Asks for copy of Karen's letter. Catherine Outried filming brought forward to next Tuesday.

Friday 5 July: Will meet with reporter David Black to plan tactics. Lord Napier has asked Question in Lords about *Inca*, 'Were STA rules broken?', and is cock-a-hoop over a letter from Lord Dunrossil, which he reads out. 'We watch with fascination your efforts, remember our conversation?' Promises details when we meet. When, I wonder? Long call from Mick Brown. *Inca* no longer Sail-Training Ship so a dead-end.

Saturday 6 July: The letter from the Prime Minister. She writes in her own hand 'My dear Miss Cooklin...' signing as Margaret Thatcher. The information the letter contains is that a Public Inquiry is to be held 'as soon as practicable'. She also informs me that *Marques* sank 'due to a sudden squall'. I remark over the phone, to David Sinclair, *Sunday Times*, that I find this statement 'naive'. My comment finds its way into the paper the next day along with an announcement that there is now to be a Public Inquiry. So far, so good. As yet I have not given any thought to the fact that I have no funds available for a barrister. Which is not surprising as my time and energy have all been taken up with achieving receipt of said letter. I suppose I had naively supposed there would be legal aid. Or that the government, in fairness to the fact they were dragged into court kicking and screaming, would have stretched a point and appointed me a brief. But perhaps they thought it was better to let the silly cow have her inquiry and see how far she gets without representation. As it happens, I was not too worried on two counts. First, because I knew a few barristers; second, and more to the point, because the press were with us and the unfairness would be highlighted.

Sunday 7 July: Ron Cooper rings, chuckling over my jibe at Thatcher's 'naivety'. Early evening, I'm about to go out, get a call from John Messer-Bennetts. Am I to be represented at hearing? Don't know. Was it me who contacted MP Janet Foukes and if not, who was it? No idea. Did I write to Thatcher? Yes. Re. carpenters, says one was dismissed, other a case of sour grapes. 'Really?' I say.

Monday 8 July: Ring Mick Brown to discuss the next move. Lord Napier rings late, he saw piece in *Sunday Times* '…exactly what Lord Dunrossil and I said, what about the hatches? What happens if a dirty great wave comes along?' He thought the crew were gung-ho: '…Oh we'd put tarpaulins over them' and went on about 18-year-olds with no one in charge and the state of the boat. Wants copies of letters from Thatcher and Ridley. He's abroad next week. Has decided not to do Canadian broadcast. 'Think I'll keep my powder dry.' He reminds me, 'We're not home and dry yet.' I ring Peter to bring him up to date. He gets such a thrill over Lord N, asks eagerly, 'Did he ring you? That's what makes it so romantic.'

TAKE NOTICE: that the Wreck Commissioner, Mr. R.F. Stone, QC, will hold a preliminary meeting in his Chambers at Queen Elizabeth Building, Temple, London EC4 on 25 July 1985 at 4.30 pm, at which directions may be given or any Preliminary or interlocutory order as to the procedure of the Formal Investigation may be made. Any person may apply for leave from the Wreck Commissioner to become a party to the Formal Investigation. Notice of intention to seek any direction, order, as to the procedure, or leave to become a party may be forwarded to the undersigned. Dated 9 July 1985. Signed The Treasury Solicitor.'

A year and a half after the *Marques* disaster, a Public Inquiry has finally been announced. The phone rings and it is Mick Brown. The *Sunday Times* have received their own copy of this Formal Notification. Mick says, 'We must have a meeting.'

'When?'

'Tomorrow if you can make it. It's less than two weeks to the Preliminary Meeting. I would like you to come in with paperwork so I can make copies. The three of us, you, me and David Black, who's coming on board, can put our heads together and discuss tactics.'

'You want me to come out to Wapping?'

'Is it a problem?'

'Not really, only could my ex come along, Ben's dad? He'd like to be part of it and I'm not too sure of my way around the East End.'

'Sure, three o'clock?'

I ring Peter to ask if he will drive me there in my car. I say, 'I don't fancy driving to Wapping, for one thing, and there are pickets there, which means I might have to leave the car outside the gates. Apparently, it gets violent sometimes.'

'OK, but be ready.' Peter is paranoid about time.

'Are you sure you don't mind driving?'

'No, I'll wear my peaked cap,' he adds. 'Well done, darling, Ben would be proud of you.'

When we arrive I am glad Peter is there. Mounted police and flying pickets are gathered around the high metal gates of News International to stop anyone from going in. As someone approaches, I wind down the window and implore him, 'I must get to this meeting, my son was killed in a disaster at sea, government are in it up to their necks, without the *Sunday Times*, don't know what I'd do. They've been shits.'

'And you think Rupert Murdoch isn't one?'

'Please! *Sunday Times* are supporting us!'

He departs to consult and returns saying, 'OK, I have a young son myself. Can't imagine what I would do if we lost him, we'll make an exception, good luck.'

I drive in, knowing Ben's sympathy would have been with the strikers.

Inside, we meet Mick Brown at long last. 'Feels daft to say "Nice to meet you" when we've spent so many hours on the phone. Welcome to sunny Wapping.'

I follow him into a vast open area, which is crammed with desks, each of which has its own computer. Ordered chaos: people rush to and fro but seem to know where they are going.

I feel awestruck to be at the centre of the beating heart of a great newspaper. On one side are glass-walled offices: in the background, the hum of presses rolling. My mind goes back to that day when David Sinclair said, 'Write that!' Lord Napier read my piece over his marmalade, reached for pen and paper and soon our personal tragedy became a news story. That is how modern media works. Now we are part of this powerful machine. I can see that Peter is affected. It took a tragedy and the loss of our son to bring us together: a tragedy of another kind. We crowd around Mick's desk, meet David Black, who, as of today, is part of the team. We shuffle papers until Mick runs a hand through his hair. 'Don't know about anyone else but I've talked myself dry, shall we head for the canteen?' As we leave Mick says, 'You know that I wish you all the luck in the world, Shirley, and by the way we've got centre-pages reserved for grand slam in October.'

It was probably just as well that we had no conception of the struggle ahead. We were about to enter the strange world of the law, where nothing is quite what it seems. I would soon become all too familiar with British Marine law – as practised by that privileged club, the Admiralty Bar.

But that is a nod to what lay ahead.

12

TO DROWN IN A BUCKET
THE HIGH COURT, LONDON,
JULY 1985

At the High Court it is the end of the working day. Lawyers have hours like schoolchildren and now in their black gowns, like busy crows, they crisscross the marble floor enrobed in their own self-importance. We look for a lift to the second floor and get out to hear voices in the corridor. It sounds more like a party than an inquiry into the deaths of nineteen people. For these lawyers, this is a jamboree. They are all from the same set of Chambers and all are Members of the Admiralty Bar. The closer we get the more celebratory it sounds. They are all on hourly rates with no inconvenient members of the public (they don't know about me yet) and are looking forward to six weeks' work, with the added bonus of sea-air. What's not to celebrate? I can only think of Bobby's voice, describing the moment of descending to the depths. How it seemed to him as if everyone was having a party and he had been left out.

Peter and I stand jammed in a corner as the meeting and greeting goes on. It seems bizarre that we are there to discuss negligence. As for this gaggle of lawyers, it is a win-win situation. The taxpayer foots the bill and if they are lucky, they will get their costs too. You could be forgiven for thinking you were at a cocktail party: it wants only waitresses bearing trays of drinks. A woman lawyer, tall, in black, and with a face like a horse, is there to protect the interests of the insurers, Lloyd's. Her presence says loud and clear that money is more important than the gallant young who died. Suddenly I cannot not bear that they are all dry and happy. Looking at their well-fed faces I want to shout, 'Do you know what this is about? Do you even care? Or is this really all about money?'

I want them to struggle to find breath, know what it is to drown. I want to show them that this is not a social gathering: that we are here to talk about death and what led up to it. Peter sees my face and says, 'Darling…' He knows me too well. What do they know of being on a ship at the dead of night and knowing you are about to die? That everything will end in those ink-dark waters? I look at those chummy men and think of my boy, descending to the depths. He would have known he was about to die. And suddenly I could not stand it any longer. 'It's their job,' I hiss, 'but do they need to look so happy?' Peter whispers, 'Take it easy, darling.'

Then I see myself – by which I mean that I seem to be watching myself. Now I am walking fast and the corridor has vanished. I am in a street I have never seen before, which is straight out of Dickens, and am heading for an ironmongers. The kind you don't see anymore. A shop with walls lined with shelves: shelves filled with boxes, boxes filled with nails and screws: hundreds and thousands of them, and ladders, standing beside the wall. And hooks. Boxes and boxes of hooks. Brackets too. Steel brackets, tin brackets, tins of fixative and wood glue. Spades and other useful implements: everything as neat and as tidy as could be. But I wanted none of these. I knew exactly what I wanted: a bucket. A galvanized bucket, shiny in the way that galvanized is shiny: dull but purposeful. Nothing plastic, not some gimcrack bucket in a bright colour but a serious bucket and brand new. One that would hold plenty of cold water, as cold as I could make it.

An old-fashioned ironmongers: a shop with a purpose, drawers full of nails and a man in a brown drill jacket.

'I need a bucket.'

'Very good, Madam. What size?'

'Large enough for a man's head, one that takes plenty of water.'

'You will require our super model,' he says.

'Yes,' I say, 'please.'

'Large enough for a man's head, you say?'

'Exactly that.'

'May I ask your purpose?'

'I want them to know how it feels to drown.'

'I see,' he says. 'Let me be sure of this: you want them to drown, in a bucket?'

'I don't care if they drown or not,' I say. 'It is irrelevant. I want them to know how it feels.'

'That gives me a clear idea. As it happens, I have the very bucket. Would you like me to wrap it in brown paper?'

We stare at each other.

'The bucket?' he repeats.

I say, 'The sea is not wrapped in brown paper, is it?'

He stares again. 'One bucket, unwrapped, nothing to pay. I wish you good-day, Madam.'

Then I am back in the anteroom and can see the bucket, even if no one else can. It stands in the middle of the parquet floor, full of water and glitters in the electric light. I will deal with each one individually, hold their heads down, one at a time, until their lungs start to burst. No doubt water will spill onto the floor and make a mess. That is the nature of water, but this is of no interest to me. I am cold, professional, forensic. I will hold their heads down, each and every one (except Mr Stone, naturally) until they splutter and can no longer breathe, until they start to choke, and if they should happen to drown, that will be just too bad. They should have chosen a safer profession. It is not the point of the exercise. I don't care either way. None of them is eighteen with their life in front of them, gentle with babies, or listens to 'Stairway to Heaven' when they should be helping with the washing-up. They have had a good innings. The point is that they should know that this is no laughing matter: that life is precious and you can lose it in an instant. I had bludgeoned my way to a Public Inquiry but now I want more: a different balance of power, not laughing lawyers on one hand and dead children on the other. Give them something to cry about, that's what my granny used to say. Ben whispers 'Bastards!' He sits on one side of me, Peter on the other, all three in a row. Peter murmurs, 'Are you alright?' I answer as if to one person but am talking to both. 'Yes to you and I am OK now.' The three of us are in the front row with Robin behind us. Mr Stone, his glasses on the end of his nose, bows his neat, grey head and opens proceedings.

'We are here to establish what happened that night and why and what lessons are to be learnt from the casualty…' (he looks round the room) '…and avoid further casualty of the same kind in the future.' He looks stern, '…and if the loss of the vessel and the loss of life was caused by fault on the part of any body or person, and if the conduct of any person is to be criticized…' (a long pause) '…we must first establish the facts.'

After dealing with points of law, he does what he calls 'housekeeping': he explains how the Inquiry will be conducted. He will have two assistants, one on either side, who will play no part in proceedings but be there as additional 'ears'– to pick up anything he might miss. All their exchanges will be confidential. Anyone wishing to be made a party may apply now, the decision whether or not to admit them is his alone: there is no right of appeal.

Counsel for Secretary of State, Nicholas Ridley, rises to his feet. This is quite a long way as John Reeder is a lanky young man, Madison Avenue in style, with curly chestnut hair and horn-rimmed glasses.

But here's the odd thing: the Department for Transport, in theory, called the Inquiry (though in fact they were dragged into the courtroom kicking and screaming) and depending how matters develop might even end up in the dock themselves. This 'conflict of interest' was the subject of a long argument over the dinner table between Robin, John and myself the night before.

'…and now we come to the circumstances in which a Load-Line Certificate of Exemption came to be issued for this vessel.' Mr Stone pauses to adjust his glasses. 'Mr Litchfield came to the Department to "see what could be done on the Load-Line front".' Suddenly there is tension in the room. 'There was a meeting with a government minister to see whether Mr Litchfield might be…' Stone pauses and the room cranes forward waiting to see what adjective he will choose. He chooses blandness, so ends '…accommodated'. There is an audible hiss of relief but moments later he says, 'And now we come to the forgery' and everyone freezes. It seems indecently early to introduce criminality. Rufus Stone narrows his eyes and as Litchfield's Counsel, John Perryman (round in contrast to Reeder) rises to his feet, Stone becomes brisk. Litchfield might well be a 'party' but he gave 'The China Clipper Society' short shrift. 'What is it?' he asks testily, as if he had spotted some dangerous insect. He makes it clear that it is the man he is concerned with and that he cannot hide behind any company, real or fabricated. Lloyd's, represented by the redoubtable Belinda Bucknall, are next. Then Jervis Kay stands for the Sail Training Association. And finally, I stand. My mouth is dry and I am trembling. The hostility is palpable and my legs have turned to jelly. I hear Ben whisper, 'Steady, Mum.'

'Sir…' I say, 'I am here to speak for my son who died on *Marques*. I need to know why he died that night and if it could have been prevented or was it…' I pause for so long that someone coughs '…an act of God?'

Mr Stone replies gently, 'No one has a greater right. Leave granted.'

Robin gets up to speak of his long association with *Marques*. He is standing behind me. I cannot see him but I sense his frustration. It was his boat long before Litchfield came along with his 'get-rich-quick schemes'. Robin tried to stop her leaving, knowing her to be unsafe. When tragedy struck, Litchfield refused to give him names and addresses. He saw no reason to contact the bereaved. It was monstrous. Peter could see I was about to burst out and says, 'Don't!'

Robin is surrounded by lawyers. I touch his sleeve and he turns to say coldly, 'I have no wish to be offensive but I cannot talk to you.'

I reply, 'I deeply regret that, Mr Cecil-Wright. I only hope these people here today realize how ridiculous this is.' As we leave Ben whispers in my ear, 'Robin's a good egg.'

13

A HORSE, A HORSE, MY KINGDOM FOR A HORSE

LONDON, SEPTEMBER 1985

If nothing else was clear after that High Court 'Preliminary Meeting' of 25 July 1985, one thing was: I needed a lawyer and needed one fast. Not any old lawyer but one who could take on the government. Someone wily and eloquent. Someone who knew the sea. A person with passion, and above all, someone who could sort the wheat from the chaff and who had a truly forensic mind. It was quite a tall order.

Lawyers come expensive. But I am lucky enough to have friends in high places. Among them are two lawyers, both Queen's Counsel. Knowing one had led to meeting with the other. I met Mike Mansfield over the dinner table when I was seeking to help a man 'inside'. 'You need Louis Blom-Cooper,' he said. Soon after I saw Mr Blom-Cooper at a Mansion House function and went up to him, saying Mike suggested I speak to him. He invited me to his Chambers. Mike was known as a rebel but Louis was an 'establishment lawyer'. This case screamed Mike but he was in the middle of a divorce and doing the Miners' Strike. So I went to see Louis.

'Yes, I was aware of the case,' says Louis. 'How sad, your son? To lose a child must be the worst thing of all.'

'And it will be a "whitewash",' I say. At this Louis gets quite shirty. 'Now Shirley, you cannot go around saying such things.'

'You don't know the half of it, the government are in it up to their necks.'

'I don't doubt that,' replies Louis, 'but that is the point of holding a Public Inquiry. Rufus Stone is an able man and you must not pre-judge things.'

'They've got half the Admiralty Bar lined up. This is a case in the public interest if ever there was one.'

It is time for the sixty-four-thousand-dollar question.

'I don't suppose you would like to represent me?' I say, trying for the casual approach.

'I'd love to,' he says.

That was the thing about Louis. You could ask a question and get a straight answer: this is unusual in lawyers.

'Of course,' I say quickly, 'there is no money.'

'You do surprise me, Shirley,' Louis says drily. 'Write to the Treasury Solicitor, stress the unusual aspects of the case and ask if my costs could be met from the Public Purse.'

'That's Miss Dewhurst?' I say, getting out my notebook.

'Yes, I believe so,' says Louis.

So I pen a letter to Miss Dewhurst and a day or so later she rings. 'Miss Cooklin, thank you for your letter. I regret to inform you that costs are not available to parties in a Public Inquiry.' That stopped me in my tracks. Surely it must be in the public interest for members of the public to make their voices heard? I asked if she had any suggestions? 'This is an unusual case, as you could be held to have activated this Inquiry. My suggestion is you write to the Department. Stress the unusual aspects of the case and ask if they would meet your costs.'

So I wrote, for all the good it did, to Nicholas Ridley, that Minister who did not even deign to answer letters from the likes of me. I could not see that going down well – the request was turned down flat.

I phone Louis back. 'Oh well,' he says, 'we'll probably pick up our costs at the other end. One of my juniors will hold the fort and I'll be there for Final speeches.' So far so good. Then, a week or so later the newspapers are full of a case of a child who was brutally murdered by her carer. What eminent figure did they choose to lead the Inquiry? Why, Louis Blom-Cooper, of course. So that is the end of that.

Time is passing. Time for desperate measures. Wasting not a minute more, I ring David Sinclair at the *Sunday Times*. 'That's too bad,' he says. 'Mr Blom-Cooper would have added lustre to your case.' Taking a deep breath, I say, 'I don't suppose the *Sunday Times* would like to fund me a lawyer?'

He laughs. Because, after all, it is quite funny to imagine the *Sunday Times* have nothing better to do than to pay the legal costs of any unfortunate who happens to appear on their pages. He begins, 'My dear Miss Cooklin...' then something occurs to him. Thanks to the follow-up piece by staff writer Mick Brown, Litchfield had taken out an injunction against the *Sunday Times*. This could prove costly. If, on the other hand, they supported me – and clearly I have right on my side – maybe it's not such a bad idea after all?

There is a pause and then he says, 'On the other hand...'

Initially, they paid for twenty days' representation. That was how it began. But as we began to make inroads into the government's case, the *Sunday Times* continued to pay. In the event, they paid to the bitter end. I say that advisedly, for, though I will not say how long the Inquiry took, as that would ruin the story, they continued to support me throughout.

Time to engage a lawyer. I ring Louis again to tell him my news. He is delighted. 'Excellent, very well done.' And the name of the young man he had intended to use as his second? 'Certainly, his name is Rupert Massey.'

Ten days later, I am waiting inside the entrance to the library at the Inns of Court. The door opens to disgorge a young man in a pinstriped suit. His appearance is conventional yet somehow suggests danger. He clutches an armful of briefs and looks me over.

'Miss Cooklin?'

I nod.

'Rupert Massey, sorry I'm late. Shall we have our discussion over a cup of tea?'

Pleasantries exchanged (over a cup of tea), we continue our conversation.

'And how exactly did you meet Lord Napier?'

'I've never met him.'

Rupert raises an eyebrow.

'He read my piece in the *Sunday Times* and wrote offering to help. He'd been on the boat hours before the disaster and talked to crew before they set sail.'

'What reason had he for visiting the boat?'

'He was in Bermuda arranging a royal visit. Said he had his own idea of what probably took place.'

'How extraordinary!'

'Yes, wasn't it? Without him I'd be nowhere and they would be getting away with it'

'Your son's name was Ben, is that right? Would that be Ben Cooklin?'

'No, Ben Bryant. I am divorced. Cooklin was my maiden and is my professional name. I changed it back after my second divorce by deed poll.'

'Your profession?'

'I am a writer but was previously an actor.'

Rupert takes out his pipe. Do I mind if he smokes?

'Please.'

'I shall need your help if I take this case.'

'In what way?'

'Well...' he makes a gesture which takes in the whole room '...assist with paperwork, hold the fort, deal with the press'. He pulls a cutting of my *Sunday Times* article from a pocket and peers at me. 'Do you often write for the newspapers?'

'The odd piece. Satire mainly. That was commissioned by the Deputy Editor. I had suggested asking Bernard Levin or Simon Winchester to write something but he told me to do it.'

'Indeed.' He studies me from beneath lowered lids. 'Would you feel competent to act as my assistant?'

'Assistant?'

'I shall need someone. Cash, I gather is limited...' he waves an arm '...check transcripts for quotes, liaise with the press, that sort of thing. I can't be there all the time. I imagine that having been an actor, it would not be a problem.' He studies my face. 'The sort of stuff a junior does.'

'I will, of course, do what I can to assist.'

He narrows his eyes. 'We will need to be a team,' he says. 'I gather we will find ourselves up against the entire Admiralty Bar...' – head to one side, he studies me – '...and you won't find that difficult, dealing with the death of your son?'

'I imagine the case won't be entirely plain sailing for you either,' I say. 'I've met that lot and was not impressed.'

'Would that be at the Preliminary Hearing?'

'Yes.'

'Mr Stone?'

'He's a professional.'

'But not our Admiralty friends?'

'I thought they were a shower.'

He smiles. 'I'm sure we'll get along.'

He goes to pay for our tea and I watch, as with painful slowness, he counts out the change. Careful with money, possibly mean, clearly bright. How will we get along? We are both strong characters and opinionated. It is on the cards that we will disagree. But I doubt very much that it will ever be boring.

As to the possible clash of personalities, I must make it my business to see that we do get along. Because he is all that stands between me and those arrogant clowns: the government's tight ship. I must make it work. Rupert is all I have.

PART TWO

THE INQUIRY

14

MARQUES PUBLIC INQUIRY OPENS
OCTOBER 1985

The government had one more surprise up its sleeve. There is an old saying: 'You can't fight City Hall.' Well, you can, of course, and many people do, but City Hall will make it as difficult as possible for you. Particularly, if as in my case, you are someone with limited resources, making it difficult for you to fight back. This was so with the *Marques* Public Inquiry. I had been told there was no Legal Aid. Then the *Sunday Times* came up trumps and paid for me to have a lawyer. Even so, with financial resources slim, I needed to keep working. But Rupert Massey, my brief, had made it clear he expected me to act as assistant cum secretary during the Inquiry, scheduled to last six weeks.

Due to the politics and the fact Margaret Thatcher's hand had been forced, she had to get the Inquiry both up and running and done and dusted. Every stop had been pulled out to make sure it could be fitted into the fast-waning year. It would begin in October and run for six weeks, until the Christmas recess. I had no sooner congratulated myself for having got this far when they produced a new ace. Public Inquiries usually take place in or around Westminster. One day Rupert rang and said, rather sarcastically, 'Have you heard the latest?'

'No.'

'They've kicked it out to the sticks.'

'Kicked what out to the sticks?'

'The Inquiry, of course. Your Inquiry.'

'What do you mean?'

'It is going to be held in darkest Devon. Plymouth to be precise. You must be prepared to stand in for me if necessary.'

I was bewildered. 'Why are they doing this?'

'Your guess is as good as mine. Probably to keep the press away.'

Rupert was proved right. Later that day I got official confirmation. It put me into a tizzy and threw up a new set of problems. I had to keep working and for that had to be in London. The coffers were depleted. Besides, my agent had secured me an episode on a TV soap, so she would not be pleased. There would be train fares and accommodation to factor in. Everyone else taking part would have their expenses met by the government. I phoned Bill Peterson and told him.

'That's too bad, Shirley. Hell, I was going to give you a surprise. I am hoping to fly over and be at your side on the first day.'

'That would be amazing.'

'Is there an airport near...what's this place called?'

'Plymouth. I expect so. I'll find out. But Bill, they're holding it in some fancy seafront hotel. I can't afford that, on top of everything else.'

'What will you do?'

'Find a boarding house. Rupert says they are doing it to keep the press away. Holding it in Plymouth.'

Bill laughed. 'I'll put my money on you every time. They'll be there. Don't you worry.'

Bill was correct. Peter, who had hoped to pop in occasionally, now had to revise his ideas. He decided to go down with me for the first day and we'd booked into a boarding house on the outskirts of town.

On that first day, we sat over our toast and marmalade and he asked me how I was feeling.

'Apprehensive.'

'Nonsense. You'll be fine. I'm looking forward to meeting your Rupert.'

'He's an oddball, but I think he'll be what we need.'

As things turned out, we were both to be disappointed. But Bill's predictions turned out to be on the money. We arrived at the New Continental Hotel on Plymouth seafront to find ourselves in the midst of a media circus.

'Bloody hell,' said Peter, 'look at them, it's like a ruddy film premiere.' He was right too. The lobby was packed. Everywhere you looked, men were setting up camera tripods or wielding sound-booms. They had come from all over the world. A Japanese cameraman fixed me in his sights, and I saw someone from the far end of the room waving frantically. It was that Canadian TV director, Catherine Outried. By now we had moved into the conference room. In the far corner, I saw lawyers gathered. They all looked furious at the media presence. Especially that formidable woman who was appearing for Lloyd's, Belinda Bucknall.

I suddenly said to Peter, 'Where's Rupert?'

'What do you mean?'

'Well, the rest of them are here – all looking furious at the press presence. But where the hell is Rupert?'

'Maybe…' said Peter, '…he's still in his room?'

'I'd better go back to the lobby and ask.'

'Don't get in a panic, darling.'

At reception I said to the clerk, 'Could tell me if Mr Massey is in his room?'

'Are you Miss Cooklin?'

'Yes.'

'I've been looking out for you. I have a message from Mr Massey.'

'Message?' Alarm bells rang.

'Yes, it came through an hour ago. He said to tell you he can't be with you today.'

I stared and then I said, 'Is that it? Nothing about when he expects to arrive?' but she shook her head. I went to tell Peter, who said, 'Bastard.' I replied, 'I know, but what am I going to do? Bill is flying in and he needs Rupert to present him to the Commissioner. We must get him to agree to Bill being a witness and that, in my view, needs a lawyer.'

Peter said, 'Bastard' again and I said, 'That's not much help. What am I going to say to Bill?'

He shook his head. 'I'd like to throttle the man.'

Then there was movement and they were just about to close the doors when I saw the Treasury Secretary, Miss Dewhurst, who greeted me, 'Good morning, Miss Cooklin, they are about to start.' Peter and I hurried into court just in time to hear Clerk of the Court, Mr Butler, say, in stentorian tones, 'All rise' as the Commissioner made a stately approach flanked by his two advisors.

'We are here to establish what happened on the night of 3 June 1984…'

John Reeder QC, all curly ginger hair and horn-rims, parks an elbow on the lectern, flexes his shoulders, swallows the last of his Fisherman's Friend and prepares to embark on a three-day peroration. Meanwhile, I am still trying to process the fact that my lawyer is not here…

'Mark Shirley Portal Litchfield served in the Royal Navy as a lieutenant for eleven years and then resigned his commission…' Reeder continues regardless. 'For a while Mr Litchfield sold swimming pools and then bought an old sailing vessel, the *Marques*. She had been built in Valencia,

Spain, in 1997 and traded under sail in the Mediterranean as a schooner…'

Next day, standing outside the boarding house, where we spent the night, I am shivering and having a nervous breakdown. Down on the seafront, at the New Continental, things will be getting underway. I am waiting for a taxi to go and meet Bill at the airport. Peter left in the small hours by the milk train and will be back at Euston station and heading to the office by now. I am composing phrases for Bill to explain about the disaster. With no one to stand up and request he be allowed to address the judge, he will have come for nothing. Then I hear my taxi coming up the steep hill. He stops when he sees me and I say, 'Thank you for getting here so quickly. The airport please, quick as you like.' Then he revs up and I try to work out how to tell a man who has just flown 3,000 miles that he has come for nothing.

On arrival I rush to the transatlantic gate. Passengers are already emerging. Head and shoulders above the crowd, I see a tall, tweedy New Englander and shout 'Bill?' He shouts 'Shirley!' and we throw our arms around each other. After a year of phone calls and anxiety we are finally on the same bit of the planet. 'That was some experience…' says Bill, waxing lyrical. 'I mean, flying through nightfall and sunrise. Let's hope it's a fitting herald of our success, eh?' This reminds me that I have some bad news to impart.

'Bill, I know this is going to sound terrible…'

'What's happened?'

'It's Rupert…my brief.'

'The guy I am looking forward to meeting?'

'Yes.'

'Is he sick?'

'No, it's a bit worse than that. He's not here.'

'What does that mean?'

'That there is no one to present you to the court. I'm sorry.'

Bill's face is a study. 'There has to be a way around this.'

'You tell me. We need a lawyer.'

'Hell, you must do it. You must present me.'

'It is not protocol.'

'But you were made a "party" at the initial hearing, were you not?'

'Yes, but I've had no legal training.'

'This is not the woman who took on Margaret Thatcher.'

'I feel like an idiot but…'

'This is for your son, Shirley, hold fast to that. For your Ben, and Susan, my sister. We are in this together. Come on.'

He is right: we have not worked, both of us, for over a year, and come this far, to give up now. He hails a taxi and as we ride into town I brief him about what happened yesterday. I explain that this is Day Two. Reeder is still on his feet, laying out his case. Somehow or other we must take advantage of a hiatus, and I will get up and ask the Commissioner to hear Bill. I am trying hard not to think about it. I am terrified of the lot of them.

As we enter the court, heads turn. John Reeder, QC, counsel for the Secretary of State for Transport, Nicholas Ridley, is in full flow. He takes in our arrival and pauses, tetchily, as the usher shows us to our seats. I bow to the Commissioner, Rufus Stone, mumble an apology and we sit. Everyone in the court turns around to stare. Reeder makes no attempt to disguise his disdain, and I want the earth to open and swallow me.

Reeder, in his natty tweeds, looks more like an advertising executive than a lawyer. But the lack of wig and gown changes nothing. I know that we are up against a dangerous adversary. This was always going to be an unequal contest – always going to be difficult, but now it has become impossible. How am I going to face the *Sunday Times*?

Reeder gives me one final, unreadable glare and turns to the Commissioner. 'Sir, with your permission, I will resume. We were about to deal with the question of how the legal breach occurred. There is no way of wrapping this up so I will not attempt to. The facts are clear. Mr Litchfield, who needed a Certificate for his vessel, enlisted the help of his MP, a Mr Andrew Rowe. Litchfield claimed to have spent over £100,000 on repairs to his vessel. He insisted his advisor, a Mr Perryman, could vouch for her. Sir, we know nothing of this Mr Perryman but it would seem that he was no more a surveyor than I am. Indeed, my understanding is that his occupation is listed as ice-cream salesman...'

Reeder's face is a study. He leans an elbow on the desk, and adopts a confidential tone. 'I believe that this letter...'

– he holds it up, turns from right to left like a conjuror about to do a trick – '…this letter, which he wrote to Mr Litchfield, is revealing to say the least. Sir, with your permission, I will now read it to the court.' Reeder positions himself and holds the letter aloft. 'We must retain our private yacht status…' – he pauses meaningfully – '…for as long as we do so, there is little the Department for Transport can do about us.' A hushed silence follows this statement and the entire room takes it in. Satisfied by the reaction, Reeder lowers the letter and looks at the Commissioner. They have arrived, rather too early, at the heart of the matter. Both men are wondering what to do now. Had a pin dropped, you might have heard it. Stone shakes his head; the complexities of the case are mounting and they are getting too fast to the problem area. Then he appears to collect himself. 'Mr Reeder, I wonder if this might be a convenient moment to adjourn?' It is clear both men found the letter hard to swallow and are wondering how to proceed. But they have had their orders from the Prime Minister. There are to be no 'ifs and buts', Margaret Thatcher was clear. It is for them to decide how to do it, but let there be no mistake, the Minister must be removed from the hook. The logical thing would seem to be to break for lunch now, but before Reeder can speak, I rise, unsteadily, to my feet.

'Sir, may I be allowed to say something?'

Reeder looks irritated but Stone smiles. 'Of course, Ms Cooklin, just so long as it is relevant to these proceedings.'

'It is, sir.'

'Then pray continue.'

'Sir, following the disaster, I was in touch with lawyers in America, who put me in contact with Commander Peterson, attached to the US Navy.'

Jervis Kay is straight on his feet 'Yes, Mr Kay,' says Stone, 'does what you wish to say have any bearing on what Ms Cooklin is trying to say?'

'Sir, my clients have the strongest possible objection to evidence from this quarter.'

'Really?' says Stone mildly.

'We have reason to believe he is related to a victim.'

'Thank you, Mr Kay. Now, if you will kindly allow Ms Cooklin to continue.'

'But, sir, he cannot possibly be independent.'

'That does not mean that I cannot hear what he has to say.'

Reeder rises, conscious of his ascendance. After all, he represents the Minister. 'Sir, who calls this witness?'

Stone says shortly, 'If you will allow Ms Cooklin to continue, Mr Reeder.'

Reeder sits, furious. I say, in a wobbly voice, 'Sir, Commander Peterson is a marine surveyor and, what is more, he is fully qualified.'

Reeder is on his feet again. 'Sir, we have reason to believe Mr Peterson is related to a victim.'

Stone says wearily, 'Thank you, Mr Reeder, that may affect the weight one gives to his evidence but does not go to admissibility. Yes, Ms Cooklin?'

'Commander Peterson has flown over from the USA, at his own expense, to give the court expert evidence. He is not only a Commander in the US Navy but also an expert on old sailing vessels. Sir, it is this area of expertise he wishes to place at the court's disposal. You are no doubt aware Mr Massey is unable to be with us today, which is why I rise in his place. Commander Peterson must fly home tomorrow but will return at the court's pleasure. Sir, I urge you to accept him as an expert witness, mindful of the fact that you yourself told us that everything must be on the table in the opening days.' Then I bowed and sat, shaking like a leaf.

'You are quite right, Ms Cooklin,' says the Commissioner, 'your request is duly noted.' I smile at him and he smiles back, as the other side glare and hiss. Bill squeezes my hand and whispers, 'Well done.' The day has been saved. But I will kill Rupert, if ever he does turn up.

As the Clerk of the Court says, 'All rise,' Bill whispers, 'Do you know something, Shirley? I felt the presence of your son in this courtroom today.' I think it was then that we both began to appreciate the sheer scale of what we had taken on.

Then, light as a butterfly's wing, something – or some-one – brushed my cheek. It had to be Ben, and I clung to that thought, as for sure we were going to need his help, to say nothing of a side-order of luck, if we were to make any headway among all these vested interests. Under my breath, I muttered a silent prayer that my errant lawyer would turn up, and sooner rather than later.

15

THE INQUIRY: THE END
OF THE BEGINNING
OCTOBER 1985

Towards the end of the third day, Reeder, who is still on his feet, flexes his shoulders and in a rather hoarse voice says, '…and that concludes my Statement of Case'.

It had begun to feel as if it might never end. Some of the evidence had come as a shock. Especially what had occurred in the Department for Transport, between Nicholas Ridley and John Perryman. It sounded so casual. Reeder did not dwell on how Ridley had openly encouraged his surveyors to break the law. But it was there in the small print if you looked for it. How could he bring himself to call this Inquiry after breaking his own laws? Of course, if it all went wrong, it would be the surveyors who would carry the can. Meanwhile, he had the unenviable task of making it sound plausible. As for Thatcher: let us not forget Ridley was essential to her plan for Britain so he could get away with practically anything. Not in a million years would the surveyors, left to themselves, have agreed. But when the Minister insisted, how could they refuse?

What it boiled down to was this. Litchfield approached his Member of Parliament for help in side-stepping red-tape, not a trivial matter. He had given permission for a boat to leave for the Caribbean without an inspection. The MP took the matter to the junior minister, Andrew Rowe, a new boy who had been in post barely a week and who was wet behind the ears. Rowe, without a qualm, took it to the Minister, who passed it on to his departmental surveyors, suggesting they take Perryman to a pub for a pint and see if he seemed a good chap. Thus instructed, the surveyors had little choice: they insisted it was Perryman's responsibility if the ship went down. They thought this covered them. When the ship did go down, killing nineteen, it was world news and Perryman became irrelevant. Someone had to answer for this. But who? It was a mess, whichever way you looked at it.

Margaret Thatcher, forced to protect her Minister, had declared that the disaster was down to a rogue wind, and tried to kick it into the long grass. Then I came along and wrote something rabble-rousing and Lord Napier took it to the House of Lords. But you tell me the Minister was not responsible and I will call you a liar. So, Reeder did the only thing possible and told the story straight-faced. What would you do, faced with an impossible task? Brazen it out. He told the truth. But everything is in the interpretation. Reeder was not a QC for nothing. Thatcher had chosen him advisedly. She had been crystal clear. He could do it any way he liked. But the Minister must be removed from the hook. Fuelled by anger, I had forgotten you can say black is white if you are a Prime Minister, and Margaret Thatcher did just that. I was a nuisance but it was easier to give me my Inquiry. In the end it doesn't matter what the evidence says. But I am running ahead of myself. I was naive. I thought if we stood up in court and told the truth, we would get justice. But enough of being wise after the event.

After three days on his feet, Reeder was about to step down to rest his voice and hand over to his second, a tubby little man called Peter Gross, who could radiate outrage better than anyone I have ever met. There had been moments in the opening days when it seemed we would never get to the end. The Commissioner, Mr Stone, had sat silent, flanked by his two advisors.

Now, as we prepare to hear evidence, Gross takes centre-stage. One moment Reeder is at the lectern, lulling us with his mellifluous tones, and the next Gross is on his feet, seething with self-importance.

'Sir, there is a matter we must consider as a matter of urgency and that is costs. Witnesses are already on their way from America and Antigua. I need hardly remind you, sir, this involves taxpayer's money. With hotel rooms and airfares to be paid for, and now we have no Counsel to speak for the other side. Witnesses will arrive and depart, with no one to cross-examine and costs will automatically be doubled.'

A concerted murmur of agreement rises from the lawyers. Stone rubs the bridge of his nose. Massey's name is not mentioned but the point has been made. The Commissioner glances at me. 'Thank you, Mr Gross, the problem is that we are in something of a quandary. One must be fair to Mr Massey. We shall have to see how we go. Much depends on when he appears.'

Next day when I turned up at the hotel, I caught the eye of the receptionist. Still no Rupert. On top of that, none of the actual crew are here. No Bobby or Andy. But I caught sight of someone I knew, Phil Sefton. He had been at the helm when the ship went down. Afterwards he stayed on in Bermuda. I had met him weeks later, at the Messer-Bennetts Memorial in Devon for their son Pete. I hurried over to say hello but he turned his back saying, 'Can't talk to you, I am giving evidence.' I know it's normal for witnesses to not talk to me but I still found it hard to accept.

The first witness taking the stand today is a hefty, six-foot young American. John Goldsmith's wife, Anthea, whispers, 'That's Barnhardt, he joined the ship the night before the race.'

The Commissioner is interested in the fact that Barnhardt, on a square-rig for the first time in his life, had been appointed 'lookout'.

'I was just told to keep my eyes open,' says Barnhardt.

'Yet it says in your deposition you went to the poop with a view to keeping a look-out, is that right?'

'Yes, but it was raining and my glasses were wet. No one said I should look for anything special. I just...looked about...I didn't really know what I was looking for. I wasn't experienced enough to make a judgement on weather. When we were hit by the wind, I didn't see it coming...'

Next, another American, Gillespie. Another six-footer who looked as if he'd be happier talking baseball. Asked about the strength of the wind he said he was not qualified to say but would describe it as '...explosive, like the air stream from a 'copter or jet'.

'And from which direction was the wind coming?'

The young man looked uncomfortable. 'I am not qualified to answer that, sir. I had just joined the ship.'

I whisper to Anthea, 'They go on about costs yet pay air-fares from the US for young men like these who had only just joined the ship. Where are the crew? Where's Bobby, Ben's best mate? He was an experienced sailor.'

'Have you looked at the witness list?'

'Not yet.'

'It's over by the door.'

'First I'll have a word with the Treasury Solicitor.'

'Do you know her?'

'Yes. She's been quite helpful up till now. But I have the sense people have been got at.'

Soon after there is a break, and I approach her. 'Miss Dewhurst, could you tell me if Bobby Cooper is to be a witness?'

She looks flustered. 'We were told he was not available.'

'Are you quite sure?'

'Yes.'

'In that case you won't object if I ring his father?'

Her face flushes. 'You must do as you think fit, Miss Cooklin.'

I go out to the lobby to ring Scotland. Wasting no time, I say, 'Ron, it's Shirley, I'm ringing from the Inquiry. I've been told Bobby can't come to give evidence. Is that true?'

Ron bursts out, 'No, it's not! We were told he wasn'a wanted.' He swears and then says, 'Ah'm reet sorry you're having to deal with rubbish like that. Ben was his best mate. There is no way he would not have wanted to speak up.'

I go back to Miss Dewhurst and tell her what Ron has said verbatim. She hears me out, poker-faced, but insists she can only act as instructed.

When I go back to join Anthea, she says, 'While you were out, that one...' – she indicates Barnhardt – '...was poking around in your papers.'

'What!'

'Look out,' she whispers, 'he's on his way over.' Then he is at my elbow pointing to my folder. 'Can I have those?'

I reply coldly, 'I beg your pardon?'

He stands there, saying nothing.

I say icily, 'I don't think we've been introduced.'

He says again, 'Can I have those?'

'I'm afraid not.'

He towers above me, puzzled. 'But...my name is there. I saw it.'

'You had no business going through private papers. You should have asked.'

'Well,' says Anthea, 'if that doesn't take the biscuit.' That was the first unpleasant encounter. Worse was to follow. I went home for the weekend feeling chastened. I had thought a Public Inquiry would solve everything but did not reckon on Rupert's defection. With no lawyer, I was up a gum tree.

On Monday morning, the receptionist again shakes her head. No Rupert. But there is some good news: Bobby Cooper's name had been added to the witness list. Amongst all the lies and equivocation, we would finally hear the voice of truth.

When I join Anthea, she asks if I'd had a good weekend.

'Spent most of it worrying. How long can I hang on? I've said nothing yet to the *Sunday Times* but must soon.'

'Give it another day,' she says. 'By the way, you missed this morning's show. A young black guy, an Antiguan, Ossie Cole, was on the stand but it was clear he didn't have much English, poor chap, and the Commissioner let him go.'

'Ossie? He was a friend of Ben's. I've a photo of them together holding the trophy. Bobby is in it too. Where is he?'

'Probably in the coffee shop'

I rush straight there to see a young black guy sitting alone and walk up to him, arms outstretched. 'Ossie, I'm Ben's mum and I'm so happy to meet you.' His face blank, he moves his chair to turn his back to me. I turn and flee. I am going to need nerves of steel for this and it is just the beginning.

That evening I went to the bar where Robin was staring at a pile of documents. 'Oh dear,' he said, seeing my face, 'no knight in shining armour yet?'

'I don't know what to do, Robin. The *Sunday Times* are meeting my costs. I will have to confess soon.'

'Did you consider representing yourself?'

I shook my head. 'Wouldn't stand a hope in hell.'

'After all this effort. Is there no way you can reach him?'

I shook my head and decided to pick his brains. 'Robin, you've known Litchfield a long time. Why do you think he did this? How could he think it would never come out?'

Robin lifted an eyebrow. 'Do you really want to know?'

'Of course?'

'It might make you wonder why you ever let your son join one of his ships.'

'There was no "let" about it. Ben was his own man. He made his own decisions.'

'Mark operates like a lot of upper-class Englishmen,' said Robin. 'His ability to think for himself was surgically removed at an early age and there is a hole where a heart ought to be. Are you ready for this?

'Yes.'

Robin took a swig of his drink. 'Then I will tell you the full story of the Cutty Sark whisky voyage and how Mark fooled ASTA.'

'You are talking about the American Sail Training Organisation, right?'

'Right. Mark would go to any length to cut costs. We were doing the Cutty Sark whisky promotion and were a bit short of cash, when he first thought of ASTA.'

'As what?'

'As a cash cow'

'You are joking!'

'No. Scout's honour. Mark came up with an easy way to make money and ever since has never held back. He used his connections and wealth to impress them. As you know, he is a Member of Lloyd's, which is how he was reimbursed for the loss of *Marques* – or its hull – within hours of the tragedy.'

'I didn't know. Go on.'

'Some years ago, he formed a lucrative association with ASTA. They were taken in by his society connections and impressed by films he showed them of his two ships in action. It was not long before he proposed to take a load of their trainees on a voyage. ASTA agreed. As a sweetener, he offered to pay the trainees' insurance premiums to the tune of $50,000.'

'That sounds barmy, why?'

'Oh, it was a con. There were no insurance policies. Mark pocketed the cash and then conveniently "forgot".'

I could hardly believe I was hearing this. 'He took a risk, didn't he?'

'That wouldn't bother Mark, forging a signature is child's play to him.'

They were making signs at the bar about closing. But there was one last thing I wanted to know. 'Are you saying Mark will not hesitate to lie where it suits him, because...'

Robin said, 'I just hope your Rupert – if he ever turns up – can beat him at his own game.'

16

RUPERT TO THE RESCUE
PLYMOUTH, OCTOBER 1985

The receptionist gives me a wink. 'Mr Massey arrived late last night, he's upstairs, thought you'd like to know.'

I flash her a smile and dash for the lift. Hurtling out to charge across the corridor, I bang on Rupert's door. This is thrown open to reveal the missing man, looking rumpled and cross, in shirtsleeves, red braces and pinstriped suit. Behind him teeters a pile of transcripts, like the famous Leaning Tower. The floor is thick with sheets of A4, scattered like autumn leaves. 'Thank God you've arrived!' he cries, as if I were the one who'd been missing.

'Well, look what the tide's washed in!'

He is straight on the offensive. 'I said I could not be here every day.'

'But not to warn me, or tell me what to do about Bill?'

'Who?'

'Commander Peterson!' I scream.

'You never said he was coming.'

'No, because I didn't know, did I? I got a last-minute phone call. He assumed you'd be here, on the first day. And, as it happens, so did I.'

Rupert runs a hand through his black hair. For all that he wears a pinstriped suit he reminds me of a gypsy. 'I am not clairvoyant.'

'No, but you could have given me notice.'

'I haven't got time for this,' he says tetchily, 'there are survivors to examine. Kindly be good enough to give me an idea of the mood of the court.'

'Hostile.'

'Court or witnesses?'

'Both. The lawyers are hostile and the survivors insolent.'

He says with an edge, 'You told me you met them at London Airport.'

'That was Andy and Bobby – neither of whom, incidentally, have been called. Ron says...'

'Who the hell is Ron?'

'His dad...they said Bobby wasn't wanted. However, I've made my feelings plain to Miss Dewhurst on that subject.'

'Who the hell is Miss Dewhurst?'

'The Treasury Solicitor, and now he is on his way.'

He says grudgingly, 'You don't seem to have wasted your time. Which survivors would we be talking about?'

'American youths, drilled to toe the party line. Oh yes, and an Antiguan boy with no English.'

'And Stone? Which way is he leaning?'

'I think he's straight. But if so, he's the only one.'

Rupert considers this. 'I suppose that's something. What about Cecil-Wright?'

'Robin is getting a rough ride.'

The Commissioner looks up as we enter the court. 'Today we have the pleasure of Mr Massey's presence,' he announces.

'Sir, I come fresh to this case. There may be two witnesses I would wish the Secretary of State to call. I shall deal with that as soon as I can.'

'Very good, Mr Massey. First you have the task of examining the witnesses that we have waiting: Denis Orde, who was First Mate, and the helmsman, Philip Sefton.'

I did not want to hear Orde's evidence. I knew for a fact he had ordered Ben to hand over his life jacket to a sail trainee that night. Bobby told me. I do not want to even go there. As Rupert confirms Orde's position, anger floods through me.

'Mr Orde,' Rupert begins, 'I believe I am right in saying you were present on deck when the capsize occurred. Can I ask if you were following weather advice on the radio?'

'No, sir.'

'Do you recall making any entries into the ship's log, before the ship went down?'

'Not that I remember.'

143

'Nothing at all?' Rupert is incredulous.

'No, sir.'

'Were you aware of what course you were on?'

'No, sir.'

'No idea at all?'

'No, sir.'

Rupert tries again. 'Can you perhaps tell me what radio station you would ordinarily be following?'

Orde repeats dully, 'Radio station?'

'I assume you were tuned in for weather advice?'

Orde says he had no knowledge of any radio stations.

'Was there anything at all you noticed about the weather, in those moments just before the ship went down?'

'No, sir.'

'You have no idea at all of what might have caused the ship to founder, is that right?'

Orde brightens. 'Oh yes, I do know that, sir.'

'What would that be, Mr Orde?'

'The ship went down because the Duradon sails were too strong.'

'Too strong?'

'Yes, sir. You see, they didn't part in the wind.'

'Then what, in your view, caused the vessel to capsize?'

'It was caused by a waterspout.'

'Have you ever seen a waterspout, Mr Orde?'

'No, sir.'

'Then what put such an idea in your head?'

'I believe, sir,' he says piously, 'that it was an act of God.'

Philip Sefton, the helmsman, is next. Rupert had warned me to be on my toes. Now, he kicks off by saying, 'Mr Sefton, it is my task to ask you some questions on behalf of the mother of Benjamin Bryant. On the night in question, I believe that you were in your bunk asleep. Is that right?'

'At two o'clock in the morning, I was asleep, yes.'

'Can you say how many sails had been taken in since leaving Bermuda?

'Eight.'

'Almost half the sail complement then. Was that because the weather was steadily getting worse?'

'They were taken in because the wind speed was rising. I don't think that is quite the same thing.' Sefton says this rather pompously. Clearly, he thinks he is talking to a landlubber.

'But would you agree that observation of wind speed is notoriously difficult at night?'

'Personally, I can estimate wind speed at night as well as in the day.'

I watch as Rupert's brow furrows. A sailor himself, he finds Sefton's arrogance offensive. 'We are talking of something which you cannot see. Do you know the difference between wind and apparent wind?'

'Of course.'

'So, did you take this into your calculations and would you agree that one of the best ways of taking wind speed without instrumentation is to look at the sea?'

Sefton is grudging. 'I would take it into account, yes.'

'Yet you did not?'

'The state of the sea and wind speed are related, but not in every case.'

'On a dark night…' – Rupert is incredulous – '…with no moon…and when, presumably, you were unable to see much of the sea? Did you take any measurement of the wind…' – he pauses as if he does not know the correct name – '…with an instrument?'

'An anemometer,' Sefton informs him. 'No, I did not.'

'So, estimates of wind speed would be based on your own experience, would that be right?'

'Yes,' says Sefton, as he walks straight into the trap which Rupert has set.

In a casual manner, Rupert now asks, 'Do you, by any chance, recollect being interviewed by the press in Bermuda?'

This is my cue to open the folder. I take out the newspaper articles which feature Sefton. But the penny has dropped and the young man is already trying to backtrack.

'If you are referring to a specific interview, you will have to be more exact. But yes, I do remember talking to the press.'

Talk? He had been all over the press there. Here, at the New Continental, I had heard him myself, promising interviews to local hacks. It was clear that he did not dislike the attention.

'Mr Sefton, if I hand you a newspaper article, could you look at it and tell me if you have ever seen it before?'

Rupert hands him the article, then asks, 'Would you say that you were happy with that piece?'

Sefton, seeing this as a trap, goes pale. 'I would not use the word "happy".'

'I am sorry,' says Rupert, 'I phrased that badly. Perhaps you remember looking at it and thinking, my God, the press twist everything?'

Jervis Kay rises. 'Sir, is there any possibility of us having copies, before this document is put in?'

'I was just about to ask whether it can be put under the copying machine,' says Stone.

But, as if he has not heard, Rupert presses on and holds up the cutting for everyone to see.

'The article is headed "Philip sets his sights on a return to sea" and you say that you were hit by a wind of enormous and freak proportions. One paragraph caught my eye. You say, "The life rafts had always been a big joke, as we didn't think they would work." Can I ask if you remember saying that, or anything like it?'

Sefton's face flickers.

'Because,' Rupert continues, 'when you look up from the deck to where the life rafts were suspended, there were braces and standing rigging, were there not? As helmsman, did you not feel that it was your duty to know what weather and wind changes might be expected? You told the court earlier that you read the night orders, I believe?'

Sefton says stonily, 'No, I did not see the night orders that night.'

'So, you took the helm knowing nothing of what weather was expected. Is that right?'

Sefton, with less bombast replies, 'Yes, that would be true.'

'Therefore, rightly or wrongly, you did not think to ask either Mr Finlay or Mr Orde for advice?'

'No.'

'You took the helm, knowing that sail had been steadily reduced since the boat left Bermuda?'

'Yes.'

'Given a steady increase of wind speed and a force 7, and with discussions about taking down even more sail going on, I put it to you that you ought to have considered it part of your job to keep a sharp weather eye for changes of wind or weather...as helmsman.'

'I would not deny that,' Sefton says stiffly.

Now I can see where Rupert is going.

'Yet this morning, you said that you were following the compass, is that not right?'

Trapped by his own arrogance, Sefton says grudgingly, 'Obviously your main attention is on the compass.'

Rupert's voice is steely. 'On a night with no moon, when it was dark?' He rocks back on his heels. 'Why would that be, Mr Sefton?'

'Because,' says Sefton wearily, 'it was my job to steer the ship and keep her on course.'

Rupert's voice is harsh. 'I am putting it to you, Mr Sefton, that your desire to keep on the compass course was motivated primarily by the fact that you were racing.'

The young man cries out, 'I deny that…utterly!'

'You had won the first leg and you – all of you – were putting the ship through as fast a pace as she could, is that not right?'

It is too late now to backtrack. Sefton replies, 'I knew that something was going to happen, I would look up and look around to see if the rain would ease or the wind increase or drop.'

'That is what you would do. What in fact did you do that night? I am asking you, I have asked you, what goes through one's mind as helmsman in such conditions?'

'I have already told you. I do not see it follows that the heavy rain was linked to a hurricane squall.'

A hush falls over the court. The Commissioner leans forward and says quietly to Rupert, 'I think you have put the point squarely to the witness.' Then he addresses the young man.

'So far as you know, there was no lookout on the poop that night?' asks Stone.

'Not in those few minutes, sir. I was on the poop and the Mates were conferring amidships.'

'It was around 4 o'clock when you took over the wheel?'

'Yes, sir.'

'And we are dealing with a period of something like fifteen minutes. Was there anyone on the port side of the poop? Anyone at all, who would regard it as their duty to keep a lookout to port and to stern?'

'Personally,' replies Sefton, 'I regard everybody on deck as lookout.'

Stone asks, with a kind of sadness, 'Do you not feel there is an advantage in persons having specific responsibilities and duties? So that you do not get a situation where a group of people all think it is the other chap who is looking out?'

Now we know for certain there was no one on lookout that night. Every person in the room knows what that led to. It was Rupert, the upstart lawyer, who asked the questions which began this. Mutterings begin and notes are passed. Peter Gross confers with Mark Litchfield; Belinda Bucknall mutters to Jervis Kay. The tenor of the Inquiry, which was all going one way, is disturbed and the stink of blame permeates the room.

At the end of the day's proceedings Rupert and I head for the coffee shop. Robin and John are waiting for us, eager to meet him. 'Finally,' John says, 'someone has given them something to think about.' Robin mutters under his breath, 'Not before time.'

Rupert wonders aloud if this is usual in a Public Inquiry. 'If this were the High Court...' he begins but Robin stops him.

'You must remember that the object of the exercise here is to get the Minister off the hook. That is the sole point of the exercise.'

'Because...' says John, '...they are Siamese twins and joined at the hip. They have, in effect, given Mark a 'Get Out of Jail Free' card and everything emanates from that.'

'Exactly,' Robin agrees.

While the three men are talking, Ben manifests to me if to no one else. He is excited over Rupert's cross-examination. 'He's really good, Mum, where did you find him?' I say, 'Through a connection, dating back to my prison visiting days.'

Ben starts to giggle. 'You once dragged Becca and me to court at half-term 'cos you had to speak up for one of your "cons". He came back to have tea with us and got lent our pocket money...' – he starts to giggle again – '...never to be seen again and you, Mum, said it was "educational".' Ben laughs fit to burst.

Then he is gone. Memories flood in of school holidays and I start to feel weepy. It is probably sheer relief at being no longer alone. Rupert has wasted no time setting the cat among the pigeons, and the outcome is anyone's guess. He may have arrived late but is certainly making up for it. Whatever lies ahead, one thing is certain: they are not going to get things all their own way. At least there is going to be a fight.

17

'GROSS AND RECKLESS ERRORS'
PLYMOUTH, OCTOBER 1985

Wednesday morning, 23 October, and Rupert's second day. We are up in his room getting ready for court. I have been down to collect yesterday's transcript, phoned to alert local press, and am now on my knees on the floor, making notes on a clipboard. Rupert, at the window, pores over his Statement of Case.

He glances at his watch. 'Better get down, Cecil-Wright is on first but I want to get the feel of the court.'

Downstairs Robin is staring at an untidy bundle of papers as Commissioner Stone addresses him. 'Mr Cecil-Wright, I have read your document. One can see the issues quite clearly...'

Then Belinda Bucknall is on her feet. 'Sir, there are one or two points I would like to raise on Mr Cecil-Wright's, if I may say, "extremely helpful document". We would suggest that any person criticised be identified. He gives us particulars of how the alleged defects in hull structure led to the failure of the hull and…'

Stone intervenes, shaking his head. 'I do not think that we want to become too pedantic. He has drawn some diagrams and he makes certain allegations about fastening and frames. I don't know if he could be any more precise than that.'

'But, sir, it is not clear to us whether criticisms are to be made.'

'As to that,' replies Stone, 'we are attempting to understand construction, so the only question I should put to Mr Cecil-Wright is whether he blames anyone. And if so, who that person is.' Then he turns to Robin. 'Mr Cecil-Wright, you have heard what Miss Bucknall said. Is it your case that any person or persons caused or contributed to the loss of this vessel? Let us take for instance the bilge key bolts. If they were replaced, they had to be bought; if they were bought, then presumably there must be an invoice. People's recollections are one thing but what was written down is important.'

Peter Gross jumps up. 'May I say, sir, we would like Mr Massey, indeed it is essential, to give us an account of what his case is, as to judge by his cross-examination of yesterday, he has criticism in mind. It would be a disaster if witnesses came and went only to discover later that a case is being made out against them.'

Rupert rises. 'Sir, I was not here on the first day and am not clear exactly what is required. Perhaps the court would like to define exactly what he wants from me.'

'What is wanted,' replies Stone, 'is one of the rules of natural justice. If a charge is to be made, then a person must have a fair opportunity of making a defence. If criticism is made, in the sense of causative fault, then that is a charge against that person. In that case that person must have proper, full and adequate notice as early as possible.'

'Sir, my client cannot blame anyone she was not there. It is not blame she thinks about. Rather she wishes me to ensure that this Inquiry look into the loss in a manner calculated to minimize the risk of this happening again. She is in no position to blame anyone, but wishes to see that proper questions are asked. One of the unusual things about this Inquiry, is that there may be allegations of some kind of...' – he pauses, searching for the right word – '... some kind of dubious background, involving the Department for Transport. As it is on behalf of the Secretary of State for Transport that this Inquiry is conducted, I make no apology for saying that it must be in the public interest that justice be seen to be done.'

'That is all very well, Mr Massey...' – Stone shakes his head – '...but is that not why the Secretary of State is separately represented?'

'Sir, as to the doctrine of Ministerial responsibility, it would seem that the Secretary of State may be compromised. In my submission, the public need to see that questions are asked.'

The Commissioner glances at the press pen, where the local scribe, whom I alerted earlier, is writing away furiously. 'It is my duty to point out that great care, very great care, has been taken for separate representation for the Department. There is no element that I am aware of, that has not been done properly.'

'Sir, I am sure no criticism can be levelled at you. However, one of the things suggested is that there has been...difficulty...in getting this Inquiry under way. It may even be that evidence of obstruction will be disclosed. My client has a desire to ensure that the public see justice done. Sir, I am not in a position to say there are allegations of fault, but if certain facts, which I will now specify, are proven, it may well be that this Inquiry will come to the conclusion they were in some way to blame for this accident. I will now specify the persons.'

Stone shakes his head 'There is no such halfway house. You must face it and your client has to face it, this Tribunal must ascertain, as best one can, what was the cause and yes, you are right, find out what recommendations can be made. But when it comes to criticism, there is no means of being mealy-mouthed about this. Those parties must have notice.' Heads nod furiously as Stone continues, 'Mr Massey, it is your examination of Mr Sefton and Mr Orde which gave rise to this. You implied some failure in duty. I am conscious here, as I am sure your client is, of the difficult ground one is getting into here.'

The silence that follows is loaded. Litchfield stops passing notes to Perry and Bucknall looks as if a thundercloud has burst. Ben starts to whisper but I 'shush' him and finally Rupert lifts his head to answer. 'Sir, there are so many areas, so many levels of responsibility, are there not?'

The two men look steadily at one another 'Sir, no one is suggesting the ship was deliberately scuppered, on the other hand there are several areas and several degrees of blame between that and a pure act of God. There are errors of judgement, are there not? These may be legitimate errors of judgement, unreasonable errors of judgement or gross and reckless errors of judgement...this is the artificial situation in which I find myself.' Rupert braces himself before launching into a very long speech, the one he prepared upstairs. It is nothing less than his Statement of Case and as this becomes clear, a frisson goes around the room.

'As concerns the owners, firstly whether the employment was of a commanding crew...'

I had wanted things investigated and now Rupert is doing me proud. He speaks boldly into an increasingly horrified silence: '...failure to properly investigate the credentials, qualifications and sailing experience of such commanding crew [and] failing to properly equip this ship for the purposes of the Tall Ships Race in which she was engaged: inter alia but without prejudice to the generality...'

He drones on, specifying hatches, water evacuation, deck surface water, navigational equipment, on and on: '... failure to disclose or sufficiently disclose such information as would enable the Department for Transport to make proper and effective judgement... failure to ensure the vessel complied with the safety and equipment regulations of coastguards maintaining jurisdiction over ports into which the vessel might be expected to be found, whether in distress or otherwise...'

The Commissioner speaks up. 'I do not understand what that means.'

'Sir, this vessel was being run over a track which took it past the United States' coastal waters. There will be a line of cross-examination that will suggest this boat did not conform with US Coastguard Regulations.'

This is not the sort of thing the lawyers want to hear. Coastguard Regulations? Whatever next?

'I will now move on to the First Mate, as a person who might be found to be at fault: allowing himself to be promoted to a position of responsibility, with insufficient experience, and allowing or permitting incorrect information as to his past antecedents, qualifications and experience to be put forward for the purpose of obtaining that employment. Against the witness Mr Sefton: failure to keep a proper weather eye open whilst at the helm of *Marques* at the time of the loss...'

Suddenly, the sound of a chair scraping on the floor causes heads to turn and the entire room turns to watch as the local hack gathers up his papers and makes a hasty exit, eager to phone in this intriguing copy.

Little does he know that Rupert has only just begun: that there is more where that came from. I want to call after him but he has disappeared. As for the lawyers, they seem to have fallen into a sort of horrified silence, as one by one, Rupert attacks every single one of them.

'Sir, the third set of allegations...concern the Department for Transport and are as follows: (a) failure to conduct satisfactory or proper procedures...or exercise discretion; (b) failure to conduct sufficient tests and research into the safety, seaworthiness and stability of the vessel, having regard to the purpose...

'Sir, the fourth group of parties, to be cross-examined along these lines, will be the Sail Training Association of Great Britain and the American Sail Training Association.'

Now it is the turn of Jervis Kay to look alarmed as Rupert goes implacably on: '...the particulars against them are (a) failure to appoint a commanding crew...(b) commencing and carrying on the race under unsuitable weather conditions...(c) failure to ascertain sufficiently comprehensive weather information...'

The catalogue continues: '...(d) failure to provide emergency, distress and safety support in the event of calamity at sea...(e) failure to observe the requirements of their own regulations; that is to say, the American Sail Training Regulations, as to...(f) age and type of persons on board... (g) the presence of intoxicating liquor on board...(h) failure to draft or cause to be put into effect sufficient or sufficiently comprehensive regulations...'

It goes on and on, until finally Rupert concludes, '...(i) failure to provide sufficient vessel support cover for ships engaged in offshore racing'.

Then, taking a look round the court, he seems refreshed and invigorated by his avalanche of accusations and rather gratified by the stunned silence in which they have been received. There is a sense that he has thrown some sort of bomb into the proceedings, at least as far as 'the other side' are concerned. The lawyers need time to re-group and to decide how to proceed.

Into this stunned silence the Commissioner speaks. 'Thank you, Mr Massey. I do not suppose everybody in this room managed to get that down, so I suggest that we consider this tomorrow when we have it on the transcript. But I do think that these come into the category of charges. I am substantially relieved about that, as, with the exception of the first, the parties concerned are present and these matters can be canvassed, although not in a critical way, as they are all subjects which we are investigating anyway.'

'That,' says Rupert, 'is what I was trying to say earlier.'

'But,' adds Stone, 'if they are being put in as a charge, then you are quite right to put them that way. That is what these procedures are for. I merely say this because one is concerned about the position of the First Mate. I understand that we are hearing from Mr Adams who took the particulars from him?'

Gross rises. 'We are, sir.'

'Then I think the sensible thing to do is that these people should be informed of what is being said. I am concerned with the state of the management. As I understand it, at the start of the race in Bermuda, that responsibility was

Mr Litchfield's. If I am mistaken, I shall be informed tomorrow morning.'

'I certainly go along with much of that,' says Gross, 'but a couple of points arise. No doubt Mr Massey will have in mind that under the Rules, if a criticism is not causative, that person shall be given an opportunity of making his defence. And may I also put it on record that there is separate representation of both the Secretary of State and the Department? Mr Massey will find that on page one of Day One of the Inquiry.'

The Commissioner permits himself a legal joke. 'Rather than nibble at these matters now, let us deal with these things tomorrow.'

Perry, fawning exquisitely, rises again. 'I hope I am not "nibbling", sir, but the court may think it important the question of when Mr Orde is leaving the country. Sir, you might think it appropriate that he be notified and likewise Mr Sefton. Sir, that is the only observation I would wish to make.' Then with a smirk he bows to the Commissioner with exaggerated courtesy and stands down. 'Thank you, sir.'

Reeder's face is a mask. 'Sir, there is the question of costs to bear in mind, should we need to hold Mr Orde over.'

'I think we might let that stand for the moment,' Stone replies. 'So far as Mr Sefton is concerned he is about to go back into the witness box. However, we have not heard Mr Adam's evidence yet and I think one must return to the basic point that Mr Finlay should never have been appointed.'

18

THE MORNING AFTER
THE NIGHT BEFORE
PLYMOUTH, 1985

Next morning in the lobby, Robin accosts me and hisses under his breath, 'Have you seen the press?'

'No, why?'

'*Plymouth Echo*,' he says cryptically, taking a crumpled newspaper out of his jersey. 'They will go mad when they see this.' He shows me an inches-wide headline: 'Marques: Barrister alleges Gross and Reckless Errors'.

'But Rupert didn't say that!'

'What does it matter? Look at the size of it.'

'Size isn't everything,' I say reprovingly.

'Shirley, stop arsing about and read the damn thing!'

The luckless local hack, unable to make sense of the arcane lawyerly discussion, had latched on to 'Gross and Reckless' and got the wrong end of the stick. Thinking, 'There's a headline if ever I saw one,' he had gone for it.

What Rupert had said, or Stone come to that, did not matter. The message was clear, and this was no longer a 'one-horse' race.

Rupert is shaving when I walk in. 'Well, you've done it now.'

'Done what?' He looks up.

'Made the headlines.'

When I show him the local paper he cracks up. 'How killing, they've got the wrong end of the stick but it's in our favour.'

'You've made Robin's day, if no one else's.'

'What a hoot,' he laughs. 'I wonder how they'll react.'

In the coffee shop later, Robin gives Rupert a thump.

'Wish I could afford you! In my view the DfT should be paying your costs.'

John says, 'You are a breath of fresh air, dear boy, and I think we should celebrate your victory with a bottle of something at lunchtime.'

Rupert's brow furrows. 'We must beware of hubris.'

'I wasn't suggesting Moet & Chandon, just something reliable and red.'

Rupert shakes his head. 'There is bound to be a backlash. What I want to know is this: can Robin throw any light on the forgery? On who might have done it or how it was connected to the changes of Captain. Furthermore, why was it decided that the refit should be done so far away?'

'It's complicated,' says Robin. 'Mark was in the middle of a divorce. He had sold a property to pay for the divorce settlement and so was forced to be out of the UK for two years to avoid Capital Gains Tax.'

'Was that why the refit was done so far away?'

'Largely.'

'Why Barbate?'

'It was cheap. As to the changes of Captain...' – Robin shrugs – '...that is even more complicated. A letter was sent to Captain De Coverley...'

'Would that be at the Department for Transport?'

'Yes. Reeder has a copy, though I doubt he plans to give it in evidence.'

'A letter from whom?'

'Leno Shaughnessy.'

'Who is that?'

'She is the sister of Gillie, the ship's cook, who was one of those killed. If you remember, when Stone suggested the letter be put in evidence, Reeder made an excuse.'

'Because?'

'Because it is dynamite. Reeder is trying to make out there was a problem in finding a Captain. That Mark took on Finlay because there was no one else. It's simply not true. Minter-Kemp was quite happy to act as skipper and told Mark so. But he wanted to be paid whereas Finlay would do it for nothing. Provided he could take along his wife and baby and half his sailing school.

'What is more...' – Robin lowers his voice – '...it turns out Finlay was quite prepared to let the ship go down and was preparing to get his wife and baby out, at the very moment the ship was hit.'

'Good God!' says Rupert

Downstairs, battlelines have been drawn and we get dirty looks. 'Mr Massey,' says Stone, 'I intend to deal with some of the points you raised yesterday...'

Gross is straight on his feet. 'Sir, before we continue, we on this side are perturbed by the way events went yesterday and think it urgent Mr Massey give an account of his case, as, sir, to judge by his cross-examination of Mr Orde and Mr Sefton, he has criticism in mind and, sir, it would be a disaster if witnesses came and went, only to discover later a case was being made out against them. It would be helpful if he could indicate exactly what his case is, and sooner rather than later. To judge by his cross-examination, he has criticism in mind. Sir, he hinted at some sort of "dubious background", something that we on this side strenuously refute. We feel he ought to be more precise in his allegations and for my part, and so far as I am aware, there is no proof at all of what he alleges. Indeed, one suspects that such accusations were made for collateral purposes – to produce a benefit from this Inquiry. It would be helpful if he could indicate exactly what his case is and sooner rather than later.'

Stone looks over his glasses. 'I would be failing in my duty, Mr Gross, if I did not point out that Mr Orde is by no means out of running for criticism.'

'Sir, criticism is one thing, but the fact remains a person is innocent until proven guilty. Until yesterday no one criticized the way Mr Orde carried out his duties and we have yet to see any proof for such allegations.'

The Commissioner shakes his head. 'Let us be a little realistic. Mr Massey, who speaks for the parents of someone lost that night, has a broad brief to see that all matters are fully investigated. Something went wrong that night and this Inquiry has been called to look into these matters. I am afraid, at the end of the day, you must accept what I say.' Then he turns to Perry. 'Perhaps you would like to give us your view for Mr Litchfield's responsibility regarding Mr Orde's lack of qualifications?'

Perry, predictably, begins to fawn. 'Sir, as to Mr Orde, the witness said that he had never met before or since a man more skilled in seamanship and sailing.'

'That is all very well,' says Stone, 'but the fact is, it now appears there was no one in charge that night and no one paying attention to the weather. Perhaps you would like to give me your opinion on that?'

'Sir, in my humble opinion,' says Gross, 'Mr Massey's allegations had more to do with getting press coverage than contributing to this Inquiry. I should like to take this opportunity of referring to his accusations that alcohol was being consumed that night. Not one shred of evidence has been produced. We on this side feel strongly about these allegations.

'Of course,' he adds with a smirk, 'I apologize for taking up the court's time.' Then he sits.

'Sir,' Rupert is on his feet again, 'it seems to me it is being taken very lightly that the US coastguard regulations were not observed. This vessel was in foreign waters, without paperwork. That alone constituted a danger. I was not here on the first day and am not entirely clear about what is required. Perhaps the court would define what he wants of me.'

Gross leaps to his feet. 'Sir, if might make bold, referring to yesterday's evidence – and perhaps I should make it clear that I speak on behalf of my learned friends on this side of the room – we take exception, very great exception, to the insinuations made yesterday by Mr Massey...' He puffs his chest out like a ruffled bird. 'So, far from there being any "dubious" background, Mr Massey would have known, had he favoured us with his presence at the start, that great care, very great care, was taken to ensure the Department and its officials should be separately represented...'

Stone sighs. It is going to be one of those days. '... Furthermore,' Gross is squeaky with indignation, '...such allegations were plainly made for the collateral purpose of producing a benefit from this Inquiry.'

Stone now is uncompromising. 'Mr Gross, let me say this. Firstly, Mr Massey has a perfect right to impute responsibility. Let us be in no doubt that so far as the court is concerned, Mr Orde is by no means out of the running. The court recognizes that Mr Massey has a broad brief, a very broad brief, to see that all matters are fully investigated...' Gross starts to rise. '...No, I have not finished yet

Mr Gross. At the end of the day you must accept my ruling...' He looks round. '...Let me ask Mr Litchfield's representative for his reaction to the allegation about the First Mate's qualifications, Mr Perry?'

Perry, who gives us to understand that he suspects Mr Massey's allegations had more to do with press coverage than adducing evidence, smirks. This produces a flurry of nods as one by one the lawyers rise to attack Rupert. James Beattie, an official at the DfT, insists there was no 'bending' of coastguards' rules. Jervis Kay suggests Massey should 'come clean'.

But Stone is in no mood for this. 'ASTA had full responsibility for the safety of the crew, and I would not wish to give the impression that we would not be asking questions. Let us be clear on that. It so happens Mr Massey has taken a critical stance. It is always open to the court to view evidence in a critical way and one must be slightly fair to Mr Massey on this.'

Overnight the pendulum has swung. But Rupert, now under attack from every direction, is too angry to notice or care.

'Sir,' he says, 'I consider it grossly unreasonable for insinuations to be made that our case was not well prepared. I would like to take this opportunity of making clear to the court that my client feels strongly about the hostile atmosphere in this room, with the exception of you, sir. I ask the court to consider this: *Marques* was obliged to pass through the maritime coast of the US and so was legally bound to comply with US regulations. Sir, no one, *no one*, seems to be taking any account of this.'

The other lawyers ignore this red herring and Stone says mildly, 'Parliament in its wisdom does not allow Legal Aid, which is partly what we are up against here.'

Gross bursts out, 'Sir, on behalf of colleagues, there must always be an objection to a person who turns up late, departs early and will return to make a closing speech.' Then Perry leaps up. 'I would go even further. When allegations are flung about in handfuls, it must be a serious matter, especially when it affects the reputation of such a respected, law-abiding, honourable citizen as Mr Litchfield.'

No one picks up on Rupert's hint that *Marques* would have been liable to intervention by US Coastguards and 'selective deafness' prevails. As cross-examination resumes, the smell of cant permeates the room.

As witness testimony begins once again, first on the stand is Ash, the young American.

'How many hours had you been without sleep when the ship sank?' asks Rupert.

'Perhaps 16 to 20.'

'You were posted as lookout, is that right?'

Ash is not sure. It might have been Barnhardt who noticed 'a canopy of cloud'. He had assumed one of the permanent crew would take note.

'So, what do you think happened…what went wrong?'

'Oh, sir,' the young man says solemnly. 'I think it was time for the boat to go.' Rupert stares hard at him. '...It was the wind. There was nothing anyone could have done.'

'You seem to be saying this boat was knocked over by an act of God, is that what you are saying?' asks Rupert, incredulously.

'Yes, sir,' says Ash.

Next is Barnhardt. 'Were you aware that you had been posted as lookout?' Rupert asks.

'No, sir.'

'I have the impression from your evidence that you went to the poop with a view to keeping a lookout, is that right?'

'Yes, sir, but it was raining and my glasses were wet. I did look about but I didn't know what I was looking for, I was not experienced enough. When we were hit by the wind, I did not see it coming.'

The Commissioner produces the following piece of wisdom. 'Experience has shown that people must be posted to specific duties, or else you end up in a situation where everyone thinks the other chap is looking out. The sea is no place for committees.'

Barnhardt is uncertain whether there was any discussion over postponing the race. So far as he knew, the Captain was below and everyone thought someone else was on lookout. Rupert asks who gave the order for the fore course to be taken down and he replies that there was no order, it was just that the Mates 'wondered' if to reduce sail.

Stone's face is a study.

Over lunch Robin is clearly nursing some grievance. 'What's got into you, Robin?' asks John. 'You look like a wet weekend in Wigan.'

Robin says, 'I should like to know why I'm being followed.'

'By followed,' says Rupert, 'do you mean by the police?'

'He didn't look like a policeman.'

'Who didn't?'

'The man who was spying on me from the bushes yesterday. There was someone, and you tell me what he was doing if he wasn't spying? I know none of you believe me.'

John mutters in my ear. 'For God's sake, get him off the subject.'

Thus commanded, I pipe up, 'Rupert, there's stuff Robin needs to tell you.'

'What stuff?'

Playing for time, I say, 'Well…about ASTA for a start.'

'No more conspiracy theories, please, Cooklin, we've quite enough on our plate.'

'But Robin knows, he was there.'

'Are you talking about the Cutty Sark whisky contract because…'

Rupert snaps, 'I am not interested in whisky, let's keep to the point, shall we?'

'Tell him, Robin.'

'I think Shirley means that Mark found a way to fund trips to Canada, after he got the Cutty Sark contract and…'

Rupert explodes. 'Stick to the point!'

'It is to the point,' I say. 'Tell him, Robin, go on.'

'Thing is, Mark would go to any length to cut costs, and it was when we were doing the Cutty Sark whisky promotion and were a bit short of cash, that he first thought of ASTA.'

'As what?'

'As a cash cow. Mark came up with the idea of "a sweetener". He offered to pay their trainees' insurance premiums to the tune of $50,000. But there were no insurance policies. Mark pocketed the cash and conveniently forgot.'

Rupert decides, 'We cannot afford to go muck–raking.'

'*Newsnight* were good for it.'

'I daresay but we are not the BBC. But, I did want to ask you about the forgery. What is your view on what Adams and Minter-Kemp will do now?'

'Pass the buck.'

Rupert turns to me. 'You met Adams, didn't you?'

'Yes, at London Airport but I didn't know about any of this then. Adams had been Ben's Captain and he told us sweet stories about Ben rushing off with the Dory, thinking he'd been asked to collect people and not take them.'

'But have you something against Adams?'

'Well, I did think it odd he should say, "What would have been the point?" when I told him about Litchfield not contacting me.'

After lunch Rupert rises to cross-examine Adams: every inch the ex-Naval man, with snow-white hair, whisky purple cheeks, cocksure and full of himself.

'Did anyone, in appointing you as Captain for *Marques*, ask for references of any kind?'

'I really do not remember,' Adams says wearily

'I understand you are going to the *Golden Hinde* now, is that right?'

'That is correct.'

'In what capacity, sir?'

'Really, sir, I do not see why I am being asked these questions.' Adams appeals to Stone. 'I am trying to give my evidence to help but I cannot see this is going to help you to find out why the boat sank.'

'Where are we going with this, Mr Massey?' asks Stone.

'I am trying to look at the procedure by which people came to be appointed and I think the question is perfectly proper.'

'How does the last assist?'

Adams says, 'It's all right, sir, I will answer. Yes, I am going as Master.'

'Going to your evidence this morning,' Rupert continues, 'you talked about the briefing you would give as Master. You went through such things as lifeboat, fire-drill and man overboard, as well as sail, set and handling?

'That is correct.'

'Is it right that you would have in your mind some sort of plan as to the kind of sail the ship might carry, under different points of the wind and weather conditions?'

'Certainly,' says Adams, 'I think my crew would know, if I had sailed with them before, exactly what I expected and what sails I was likely to carry and in what circumstances.'

Now Rupert, with infinite guile, leads Adams from sailing technique to documentation, to who would sign documents, and then on to whose responsibility it was. Then to who might have written the Master's forged document, or typed it.

'At the end of the document it says "John Adams, Master", is that right?'

'I would think exactly so.'

'So, why did he put your surname down?'

Gross pipes up. 'May I ask, through you, sir, where all this is going? These inquiries are rather expensive and details as to who typed what may be fascinating but not of great assistance.'

Stone says, 'Do you think you could put to the witness, parts of the document? This does not need a speech.'

'Of course I can,' answers Rupert, 'but it is unfair to the witness and I thought he would want to read it to see if it is his.'

'Could you put some relevant passage to him and let us see how we go?'

Rupert fusses with the document. 'Very well, on page 21 we have: "Continual complaints have been received about delay, late arrivals and late departures and lack of information, and incorrect information." What do those words mean?'

'I would imagine being told that we were going to do one thing and finding we were doing another.'

'Do you not think that "misleading" might have been better?'

'If I had thought it was going be produced in court, yes.'

'The fourth bit mentions "lies". Were lies told to you?'

'Not so far as I know. I trusted the word of everybody.'

'All the time?'

'Well, if somebody told me it was Tuesday and it was Wednesday, I would not hold that against them.'

'Did there ever come a time when you did not trust the word of somebody?'

'Now we are getting on to who was in charge of the management of this ship, are we not? I believe you have an ownership dispute and I do not want to get involved in that.'

The Commissioner intervenes. 'I do not have that problem, but I must keep an eye on the management!'

Gross breaks in. 'Really, sir, Mr Adams is an innocent person and there is always the question of "costs" to consider.'

'Sir, I must protest.' Rupert is furious and now lets rip. 'This Inquiry took an inordinate amount of time to get underway. I am half-minded to put my client in the box, for she it was who tirelessly wrote letters and spoke to America, in an attempt to see that these events were properly investigated…' – he looks round the room, because while he's at it he might as well leave nothing out – '…and sir, it must be said that she has not been accorded the respect in this courtroom she deserves. She is a mother, whose son was needlessly killed. There was an attempt at the start to paint this tragedy as an 'act of God' but it is clear to me, that a doubt hangs over seamanship at the time this vessel foundered, as it does over documentation and over who is telling the truth. We are here today only because she refused to give up and I am minded to put her in the box, so that she can tell the story in her own words, since my handling of this case seems to cause such exception.'

There is an uneasy silence but Stone is quick to pour oil on troubled waters. 'That will not be necessary.' Rupert is proving to be something of a handful

'Perhaps now we can proceed to the evidence of Mr Martin Minter-Kemp.'

Minter-Kemp is blunt. 'The safest ship on earth would become unsafe if handled by someone who does not take the right action at the right time.'

'You regard those seas as dangerous or unpredictable, do you?'

'I have grave reservations.'

'You had arguments with Mr Litchfield over repairs, is that right?'

'I had concerns, yes.'

'Concerns over the seaworthiness of the vessel?'

'Not at the time. But I am very concerned now. That is a dangerous place for mariners. The squalls are sudden and unpredictable and come from different quadrants of the compass, often within minutes.'

'Let me ask you this, would you have been sleeping soundly in your cabin during such weather?'

'No, I would probably have been sleeping on deck.'

Perry jumps to his feet. 'Suppose it was someone without your idiosyncrasy, would you have been sleeping soundly?'

Minter-Kemp is terse. 'I doubt it. I believe that a mariner must expect the unexpected in that part of the world.'

''Sir' – Rupert can no longer contain himself – 'we have heard a wealth of evidence, of sloppy seamanship, people not knowing their duties, of things minor and major that went wrong, of a dereliction of duty by the Department for Transport, whose evidence we have yet to hear. Sir, I find it incredible, truly incredible, that the Secretary of State can say that there is no prima facie evidence leading to causative criticism, quite incredible.'

Stone goes red. 'You need not make a speech about it, Mr Massey.'

But Rupert is past caring. 'Sir, nobody here is looking at primary facts and making anything other than benign and benevolent inferences.'

Stone's voice is chilly. 'You will be a lot more persuasive to this Inquiry if you are slightly more polite about it.'

At the end of the day, good news regarding my conversation about Bobby with the Treasury Solicitor has filtered through and Bobby has now arrived to give evidence. At last we will hear the unvarnished truth about those last moments.

19

BOBBY
PLYMOUTH, OCTOBER 1985

Bobby looks apprehensive: he is here to relive the most terrible night of his life.

At London Airport, he had looked at me gravely when I put my hand out, like some woman at a cocktail party, to ask if he knew Ben. 'I am his brother,' he had said, and we had put our arms round each other and wept. Now, taking the stand, he looks barely old enough to have left home. I try not to think of bones on an ocean floor, stay behind a pillar, watch and listen.

Gross leads off. 'Mr Cooper, thinking of Friday the first of June...'

Bobby comes in at once. 'A very nasty evening, it blew very hard that night and made an interesting evening for us because we were stern to the *Hamilton Princess* – I believe it was blowing 45 to 50 knots – and the anchors were dragging so much that we had to call in a tugboat. Two or three of the boats along the dock had anchors dragging and all had lines out to each other. It was chaotic. A tugboat was called and we laid out an extra anchor on *Marques*, which helped pull *Inca* and made all the other boats along the dock more secure.'

'Was the change in the weather sudden?'

'Yes, I believe it was blowing force 3 to 4 in the morning and there was a big swell running.'

'Did you,' asks Gross, 'think that in such conditions the race should not have started?'

'It depends, the sea state was rather unfriendly and put virtually everybody out. Our crew was decimated down to a third in size of actual, useful people.'

Gross asks a leading question. 'Let us suppose someone had asked you, would you have been in favour of starting the race at that time?'

Bobby looks worried. 'I would not have liked to take a load of green kids out sailing in the nasty seas that were out there, not if I'd been asked, no, which does not mean I'd have said, I thought we should not start the race, or that I would not like to, but I am sure none of those kids, that first day, enjoyed it. It was supposed to be a sail training race but they sure didn't learn much besides which side the lee rail was.'

'And if you had been helmsman, would you have had a lookout on the poop?'

'Not all the time, no.'

'Why not?'

'Because the helmsman can usually see from the stern.'

'We have heard evidence the crew were seasick. In your view did this have a bearing on what happened?'

'It was not the crew so much as the trainees. Most were seasick, they were used only because we were short-handed. It was a bad time for a training ship to be out with that sort of weather. I reckon they should have waited to start.'

Bobby was the very first to say in plain terms that management of sail might have had something to do with what happened.

Jervis Kay steps up and asks, 'If you had taken in the forecourse, what is your view? Could the vessel have survived the wind that hit you that night? After all, you know the ship.'

Bobby replies, 'My gut reaction is that we would have stood more chance.'

Was this why the Treasury Solicitor did not want Bobby to come and give evidence? All the lawyers seemed to regard Bobby as key: the Americans, Ash, Barnhardt, Gillespie, were all raw recruits: Orde, the First Mate, seemed pretty clueless, going by his evidence. Sefton, on the other hand, had come over as too cocky, but Bobby, they sensed, was a seaman, so they threw their questions at him and Bobby walked a tightrope. The probing went on and on. I tried to imagine Ben standing in the witness box with that weight on his shoulders: if only it could have been him.

Kay wanted to know Bobby's opinion about the change of sail. 'Let us suppose that the forecourse had been taken down. In your view would that have made a difference?'

'Yes,' Bobby says, 'quite definitely. My gut reaction is that we would have had more chance.'

'Then let us take this further. I think you said earlier that from his vantage point the helmsman was, of necessity, keeping an eye on the weather, so can I ask, in your view does the person on the helm at night have a difficulty?'

'There is always some difficulty. What I was trying to get at is that, as helmsman you are constantly looking around, to some degree, everyone on a boat is always looking around.'

Kay changes tack. 'So was it dangerous in your view to start the race?'

'On hindsight, I must agree with you.'

'You are not agreeing with me. I am asking you a question.'

Bobby becomes flustered and wants it over with. 'Sir, I do not think I am in a position to say, not as things were then.'

'Really? Because in my view that is exactly what you seemed to be saying, and it is not really fair, is it, to ask those who were making a decision to postpone a race for all the ships because, on one vessel, some crew might be green?'

'One vessel?'

Kay was being gung-ho. 'Individually, it was a matter for the Master of each vessel, surely?'

Bobby did not know what to make of this. He had tried to tell the truth as he remembered it, about a night he would never forget and now looked to the Commissioner for help. 'I would not like to comment about that.'

The Commissioner sees it is time to intervene. 'Who was, so to speak, taking the lead in decision-making?'

Bobby looks drained. 'There was no one at that point. It was more of a discussion, really.'

Rupert rises. 'Can you tell us,' he asks casually, 'if there was a bar on board this boat?'

The lawyers react. Papers are shuffled like a rustling of leaves. Bobby sees no alternative but to tell the truth.

'Yes.'

'Was there alcohol on board?'

'Yes.'

'At the time she was racing?'

'Yes.'

'And you were called out to go up on the yard arm to take down sail?'

'Yes.'

An odd kind of silence falls, for everyone senses that for shock evidence like this, some sort of private meeting is needed and they are on very thin ice. Rupert takes a pause, to make sure this has sunk in, and then asks Bobby to describe the moment the ship began to heel. I had expected it, knew this moment must come, but it was a shock just the same. To take the sting away, Rupert asks the boy if there had been a change of helmsman, but in fact, nothing is going to help and Bobby looks a lonely figure as Rupert asks him to tell the court, in his own words, what happened next.

My neck felt dislocated and I could not even turn my head, my breathing suddenly felt laboured. Yet it was not as if I was hearing it for the first time. I had heard it all upstairs at Grafton Road, that night in early June, when Bobby and I had been alone and he had described the moment the ship sank, the moment his 'brother' (who was also my son) was swallowed up by the ocean. Now I must hear it again in this hostile courtroom: relive again, the moment of my son's death.

Bobby's voice is clear, but he sounds tired. 'At 3.44 I went up on deck for my 4 am watch. Phil had just been relieved at the helm…' – the room settles into an uneasy silence – '…it was still choppy and black. I could not see much, with night-sight. Then, just after 4 we were hit by the most tremendous bang and the boat…' – he pauses – '…it was not a knock down, it was gradual, but she seemed to heave to the side, and then…well, she heeled over, put her bows into the wave and was driving, and driving, slowly at first, and then at a tremendous rate, and she seemed to sail down, and over and under.'

My neck goes stiff again. I must not miss a single word but there is a dreadful inevitability about it. He had no choice but to relive the worst moment of his life when he watched his home disappear and his friends die. I looked for Ben but if he was there I did not see him.

'I was forward and ran back, down the leeside. I shouted to Phil and got a shout down below. I was going forward back aft, up on the poop deck…and…second by second the water was getting up, higher and higher. Then I shouted to Phil to come out on the weather side and we tried to go for the forecourse to spill the wind, we struggled but could not get it off, and now we were working underwater, we...tried to cut it but got swamped, then suddenly I got caught up inside the lee shrouds, I saw Andy and Ben and I'm not sure who else, they were sitting on the engine hatch, and I watched as they...slid into the water...'

As I'm hearing this, the world is suddenly dark: there is a wall of water. It enters the lungs and the weight is terrific: everything is in slow motion and...memories of life...love...Tine, her smile...this is the end...something I never thought would happen, or not in this way. I thought I would go as a bird and soar into the sky...the water is pressing...and pressing...the light falls on Tine's hair...

Bobby is still talking. 'I was halfway up inside the shrouds when finally, she started to go down. When I think about it, sometimes it seems like half an hour and sometimes just seconds, but as to the actual time I can't say, I just went on going down and down until I got tangled in the clews, I struggled and then...you stop struggling. I suppose I began to float up to the surface, the air in my waterproofs carried me up and I saw her, the ship, watched as she slowly began to sink...and then there was nothing. I must have swum to a lifeboat but I don't remember, I was feeling sick, cold, she went on disappearing. I knew she had gone, that Ben and the others had gone, but it was too late and I was shivering. I think I was sick but I don't remember, just the smell on my clothes…'

The pillar shielded me but there was no way I could stop. I knew I must stay calm and focused, that I had a job to do, but the tears ran and there was no way I could stop them. Suddenly we were breaking for lunch. When the room was finally empty, I could escape. I knew Rupert would be furious but it had caught me unawares. I was helpless and just wept.

After lunch I went out to stand at the iron rail and look out to sea. It was cold and I did not have a coat. As my teeth chattered and my cheeks stung it brought me back to reality. It must have been at least an hour before I came back and the desk clerk called out that there was a note from Rupert, just three words: 'We must talk.'

I took the lift up, knocked on his door. The moment I was inside he launched into me. 'You're no bloody use to me if you give in. You're here to do a job and you are playing into their hands. You should know by now this is a war zone…' Then he stopped and shook his head. 'You should never have started this if you can't hack it.'

I said I knew he was right but hearing Bobby's account of the moment of Ben's death described in that hostile court, had undone me. I repeated that he was right and said it would not happen again.

20

THE BIG PUSH
PLYMOUTH, OCTOBER 1985

Outside it is black as the pitch on the hull of a boat. Inside Rupert's room, I was sitting on the floor, leaning against the bed, eyes closed, listening to him talk to Bill, across the Atlantic.

'Yes, it arrived yesterday…no, very clear…the curve of the wind…I do understand…yes, it was regrettable that I was not here when you came, but Stone seems to have grasped the point…hostile but I have made some headway with the Commissioner…yes, that's right…it's hard to gauge…but I am hoping that he will grasp the importance of your evidence.'

Then Rupert, glasses on the end of his nose, listens intently, nods, as a strand of greasy black hair falls across his brow.

'And to you…' he says and puts the phone down.

'What does Bill say?'

'That he has put the drawings and the calculations in the post.'

Next morning finds us bleary-eyed in the coffee shop with Robin and John.

'So what does the great man say?'

'Oh, he'll come, no problem there, the trick is to get Stone to call him.'

'And just how do you plan to do that?' asks John

'I shall get Reeder to do my work for me.'

'How exactly?'

'I am not entirely sure. In the meantime I intend to concentrate on weather.'

An hour later, Rupert is on his feet. 'Sir, my client's case is that a weather watch, whether by sight or radio, was not maintained by the Master and First Mate. That allegation remains. Furthermore, I should like to know why the guard ship, the *Assiniboine*, was allowed to go to the aid of another vessel without anyone being alerted.'

Jervis Kay stands. 'It is not a norm to have a guard ship.'

'Then why was one allocated?'

'Are you asking me, Mr Massey?'

'Since you are the one making the allegation, yes, I am.'

'There was a guard ship, but she was called away.'

'A guard ship called away is no longer a guard ship.'

There is an uneasy silence. Then Kay says belligerently, 'It is not in the rules and there was no concern about the weather at the time.'

'Ah yes...' says Rupert, 'I was coming to that, can someone explain to me why there is no weather information in the papers issued to Counsel?'

'I would have to say, sir,' Reeder replies, with dangerously bad grace, '…because we did not consider it of the first importance.'

This is what Rupert has been waiting for. 'As it happens…' he says, waving a sheet of paper, '…I have here an article, published by the US Navy Institute, which I should like to put in as evidence. This suggests that there was considerable reason for concern.'

'I should very much like to see that,' says the Commissioner. 'Has it been copied?'

For Stone is a man hungry for evidence, for what he can see or test (preferably printed on a sheet of A4), a rational man, mired in a story which is beginning to sound like a concoction of rumour and lies.

Rupert says airily he has not had time to make copies. Then adds silkily that he had assumed the Secretary of State would produce evidence on weather. Everyone turns to look at Reeder.

'Mr Reeder,' says Stone, 'what is your response?'

His response reeks of hauteur. 'Sir, my response is that Mr Massey is at liberty to produce his own evidence.'

'That is all very well, Mr Reeder, but it is not just Mr Massey who has concerns. The court does too. Why are there no weather documents available?'

Reeder flushes. 'We…did not anticipate such a searchlight being shone on this issue.'

That 'we' says everything. You can almost see Thatcher and Ridley nodding. Stone, a decent man, mired in a situation which is none of his choosing, says through gritted teeth, 'But it is not just Mr Massey who has concerns, the court does too and I should be obliged if you would be kind enough to inform us why no weather documents have been made available.'

'Sir, I feel bound to remind you we are already falling behind, an extension has already been mooted and now we have an expert witness, Sir Rae McKaig, who comes here, at taxpayer's expense, waiting to give evidence from the Race Organizers.'

'Very well, Mr Reeder, we will proceed, but I should like to express my dismay that such vital evidence is lacking, with so little excuse offered.' Then Stone turns away and goes into a huddle with his two advisors.

Ben, who has reappeared at my side, says, 'Blimey, I thought it was only anarchists who threw bombs!'

But Rupert has seen another opening and says brightly, 'On the subject of weather, sir, I do have a helpful suggestion. Lord Napier was on board *Marques* just before her final and fatal voyage. He may be able to assist.'

Stone shakes his head. 'Thank you, Mr Massey, but Mr Reeder reminds me, we are already lagging behind.'

Rupert insists, 'Sir, with respect, it was not only Lord Napier who was on the vessel, but also the Governor of Bermuda, Lord Dunrossil, and it would appear that weather was a matter of discussion, and sir, this cannot be lacking in importance.'

Reeder snaps, 'Any such evidence can at best be anec-dotal and I am bound to add that the Secretary of State [by which he means himself] is not minded to call this witness and sir, we have Christmas staring us in the face.'

'Sir, he was one of the last people to see the vessel, and in my submission it must be useful to hear from him. Besides we have on record his statement that the vessel appeared top-heavy...'

Reeder snaps, 'Hearsay!'

'...and if I might make so bold as to say, sir, evidence as to stability has been sadly lacking to date.'

'Stability...' Stone repeats, '...that is right, why have we heard no evidence on stability?'

Now Rupert plays his best card. 'We, on this side, do have an expert witness ready to come over to give evidence. I refer to Commander William Peterson.'

Kay is on his feet. 'We would object to this witness.'

'On what grounds?'

'He was related to one of the deceased.'

Bucknall rustles to her feet. 'I was just about to say the same thing.'

But Stone won't have this. 'Lack of independence might affect the weight one gives to the evidence but does not go to admissibility. Mr Massey, can you determine if the witness is still prepared to come to the United Kingdom?'

Kay tries again. 'Sir, if I might say...'

'No,' says Stone calmly. 'No, Mr Kay you may not. I am not minded to hear any further objections on this score. In my view, this is what these inquiries are about. We spend a good deal of time finding fault but here, we have something which is the very meat of recommendation, on safety for the future.'

Reeder again. 'May one ask who is to call this witness?'

Stone says shortly, 'The court will. And now I would like you all to bear in mind that there is a great deal of evidence still to be heard.'

'Exactly, sir, you see my difficulty.' Reeder rocks back on his heels.

'Indeed and I am anxious we should waste no more time.'

'Sir, I am grateful,' says Rupert. 'Our next witness is Admiral Sir Rae McKaig, who speaks for the Race Organizers.'

McKaig takes the stand: as far as he is concerned there was no cause for alarm over the weather and he disagrees with Lord Napier.

'Was it right,' asks Rupert '...to start the race in near gale conditions?'

McKaig was not aware of bad weather.

'There is the question of the baby on board, in contravention of STA rules, and I would also remind the court that in addition we have the problem of the ship in trouble.'

McKaig looks mystified. 'What baby, what ship?'

'Sir, the Captain's baby. Were you not aware that a vessel, not a million miles away, was already in dire straits? I refer, of course, to the *Mirabel*.'

The Admiral appeals to Stone, 'I came here to give evidence about the race and feel I am being attacked.'

Kay jumps up. 'Sir, what relevance has this to *Marques*?'

But Stone opts for Rupert. 'Mr Massey has a difficult job to do, and in my view, there is nothing untoward about his questions. I must remind the court we are dealing with a fatal incident, in which nineteen people lost their lives. Mr Massey is not the only one who wants answers.'

Now it is Bucknall's turn. 'We have heard from Mr Sefton the weather was unexceptional. So anyone now suggesting the race was started in stormy conditions is talking through his hat...'

But McKaig would not go as far as that.

'When and under what conditions would you postpone a race?'

'Well, if say the weather report on Friday had been totally bad for the two days in question,' says McKaig.

Kay jumps in. 'It is ridiculous to suggest the Sail Training Association should have checked the certificates of every member of the crew.'

'Objection,' snaps Rupert. 'Counsel is leading the witness.'

Kay lobs another ball. 'Under what conditions would you call for a race to be abandoned or postponed?'

'Well, I can think of several scenarios.' McKaig purses his lips. 'If say...the weather report on Friday had been totally bad for the whole of the two days in question, that might be a reason.'

Kay has not finished. 'Would you not agree, sir, that it would be ridiculous to suggest the mere presence of a baby on board could be held to have induced tragedy, as Mr Massey suggests?'

'I have already warned you, Mr Kay, about leading the witness,' Stone says, 'and since you bring up the subject, I will give you my view and it is this. The presence of each person on board, particularly those who lost their lives, is relevant. Mr Massey happened to raise it in this form, and I am rather pleased he did.'

On points, Rupert is now in the lead, but the 'entente' between him and Stone is fragile and may be nearing its end.

Recess is called and we head for the restaurant. As we sit, John says, 'It was masterly the way you had Stone eating out of your hand and that was a clever way of ensuring Commander Peterson's evidence gets heard.'

'We are walking a tightrope here and I must bank everything on weather and the forgery for the moment,' says Rupert.

'Do we even know when the Inquiry is likely to restart, after we finish here?'

'No, but in my view, we are looking at months rather than weeks. There is talk of somewhere in London.'

Next day the tone changes again. Clearly there has been discussion between Reeder and Stone overnight; the

Commissioner says they must get ASTA out of the way while Reeder insists they concentrate on 'live issues'.

Rupert is on his feet before he has finished. 'I am astounded that the Secretary of State can say that, since we have still not had the weather evidence we were promised...' but Stone stops him. 'Do not make a speech, Mr Massey.'

'Sir, I was not going to, but we were promised weather information and it has not been forthcoming, it must remain a live issue. What is the public to think? We were convened to give answers and when people hear how lightly we have dismissed this tragedy, parents will consider whether to send their children to sea...' He pauses. 'Surely it must be a serious matter that after all these weeks in court the Inquiry has not yet fully considered the safety aspects that led to the tragedy? The American coastguards were clear that any vessel in their waters was legally bound to adhere to certain standards.'

'We are not American, Mr Massey,' says Stone, 'and I am completely against you on this and again feel obliged to remind you on costs.'

Rupert bursts out, 'Sir, I find it incredible, truly incredible, that the Secretary of State can say there is no prima facie evidence leading to causative criticism, quite incredible.'

'You need not make a speech.'

'I am not making a speech, I am making my feelings felt. I am quite simply amazed that nobody here is looking at the primary facts.'

'You can make whatever submission you like, at the end of the day, but you will be a lot more persuasive in this court if you are slightly polite. I have assisted you as a novice in these proceedings as much as I possibly can.'

Rupert knows he now has nothing to lose and says, 'I still say, sir, that radio watch should have been maintained. That the *Assiniboine* should have let others know they were going to a ship in trouble, and sir, I would remind the court that there are still questions to answer on pirative law!'

The outburst is greeted with a stunned silence. Rupert, looking round the court, decides to go for broke. 'Was it a breach of regulations which contributed to the loss or which give rise to the breach? It is a requirement of the US Coastguards that all vessels have watertight bulkheads. We know for certain *Marques* did not and must ask ourselves, firstly, why the ship went over, and secondly why she sank in 45 seconds?'

Stone's face is purple. 'Mr Massey, we have a great deal of material still to get through and I must remind you that we are not a court of law looking to find liability.'

Their 'entente' is over and Rupert is being thrown to the wolves. Stone turns away, saying crisply, 'Now, where do we go?'

I recall Bill's words, in a letter received yesterday. 'I felt your son's presence in that Inquiry room.'

We are not here just to consider people breaking regulations or even a forged certificate: nineteen people lost their lives, so surely someone must be answerable for their deaths?

21

CHICKENS COME HOME TO ROOST
PLYMOUTH, OCTOBER 1985

The day has finally arrived for Mark Litchfield to be examined. Reeder, who must grasp the nettle first, clears his throat and kicks off. 'Mr Litchfield, can you tell us what the thinking was, if there was any thinking, about the need for a Load Line Certificate in 1980?'

Litchfield, who seems surprised to find himself in the box, answers vaguely, 'Quite honestly, I don't recall. I suppose it is possible the DfT might have wanted some sort of certificate, but it did not seem all that important. We were not even sure what was meant, or if one was supposed to take these regulations totally seriously.'

The Commissioner leans forward. 'Mr Litchfield, can you tell me this, when you got that letter in '75, from a Mr Whitehead in the Department for Transport, saying you needed a Load Line Certificate, what exactly went through your mind? Did you think, "Goodness me, what can all this be about?"'

Litchfield relaxes, the Commissioner is talking his language. 'Well, exactly, sir, quite honestly, at this stage I doubt that we even knew what a Load Line was.'

But Reeder won't have this. 'Surely it was crystal clear the letter constituted a clear statement by the Department that your ship needed a Load Line?'

'I suppose one could say that.'

'Then would it not be fair to say it was probably something to which you should have paid attention, but did not? Would that be right?'

'Possibly....' – he ponders – '...by the strict letter of the law...probably...yes.'

'And that letter was clear to you, was it?'

'Yes.'

'Then did you seek to contact a Mr Darlow?'

'Mr Darlow?' Litchfield sounds incredulous. 'I am sorry, I do not recall, it did not seem important, I have no recollection...well, put it this way, the DfT might say that you need a certificate but without really meaning it, or expecting me to do anything about it, if you see what I mean.'

Reeder, tight-lipped, says, 'Let us move on, shall we?' but Stone comes in. 'Mr Reeder, I think he should have the opportunity of answering the question, even if his answer does not relate to the question you asked.'

We seem to be drifting into the realms of fantasy. Now Stone leans forward earnestly. 'I have noted you had reached a stage where the letter of the law was being read to you and were quite put out. Can I ask if you have anything to add to that?'

'Thing is...' answers Litchfield, 'I think I may have slightly misunderstood the question.'

A long look passes between Reeder and Stone, who now says, 'That does not matter, it was just I wanted you to finish what you were saying, even if it was not related to the question Mr Reeder had asked you.'

Some of us have begun to feel we are in *Alice in Wonderland* territory. Litchfield seems to catch up and says brightly, 'But, sir, that is exactly what prompted me to write to the MP. Then that brought about the meeting at Sunley House on the 9th of July.'

Reeder, who is showing signs of strain, turns to Stone, wearily. 'Sir, if it is convenient, we will come to that at two o'clock,' and with a sigh of relief the court stands down.

We are upstairs in the office, having a 'council of war': tomorrow or the day after, it will be Rupert's turn to ask the questions, so we have skipped lunch as there are things to be discussed.

'We must try to find out why he left the Navy. Did he jump or was he pushed?'

'What if it's neither and he just felt like a change?'

Rupert dismisses this. 'His grandfather is an Admiral and the Navy is a career for someone like Litchfield, not a job. Besides, no one takes a commission to bow out after eight years. The real question is, was it something murky? That won't be easy.'

'Do you want me to get on the phone?'

He shakes his head. 'They don't exactly dish out this sort of information, but if we could dig up some dirt…' He has an idea. 'I might ask a tame MP to look into it.'

I have an idea of my own. 'What about Lord Napier?'

Rupert says it would be a mistake to involve him. 'Besides,' he says, 'your job now is to comb the transcripts.'

'Looking for what exactly?'

'How many times he (Litchfield) says "don't remember" or "can't recall". He never gives a straight answer.' He gets his pipe out, considers. 'Yes, I think that's where you'd be best employed, and it won't be wasted because we'll need it for the Final Speech anyway.'

The very idea that day will come gives me goose-pimples. 'Will we ever get there?'

'It won't be here. I can tell you that. We're over-running as it is and there's Bill and Lord Napier to do, but right now I need numbers so I can say, "Mr L said twenty times, 'I don't remember' or 'I can't recall.'"'

I said I would get weaving and asked how he thought Robin would fare.

'He's got to hold his nerve. Robin's got four times Litchfield's intelligence. What I worry about is Bucknall steaming in.'

'What's it got to do with her?'

'You might well ask, but don't forget they are Siamese twins because their interests go in the same direction. Stone knows that but will never admit it. You must remember this Inquiry was set up to protect the Minister and that's the tune they are all playing to.' He looks at his watch. 'Come on, we'd better go down, grab a sandwich and get back in there.'

After lunch we are back in the realms of 'don't remember' and 'can't recall' until Reeder feels forced to ask Litchfield if he ever broke the law or ever said anything that could be construed as untrue. Litchfield returns to his theme: all he had ever done was to approach his MP and ask for assistance in evading red tape.

'So would it be true,' asks Reeder, 'that in making that request you said nothing untrue?' Litchfield certainly hopes so and offhand cannot recall any such thing.

'Then are you not surprised that the DfT should suggest something illegal went on, or that you were in danger of prosecution?'

'Well,' says Litchfield, 'we did not really see it as a problem...'

We all wait to see what he will say next.

'...after all, we could always have transferred to another flag.'

The court gives a weary sigh.

Reeder and Stone have decided there was nothing wrong in his making an approach to an MP (though

Reeder does ask if anything 'untrue' was said, or the truth 'varnished'). Litchfield stoutly denies any such thing: he had sailed that vessel over mountainous seas and come to no harm; '…there would have been no point…' he opines, '…because we could have transferred the flag to, say the Congo. It would have been quite easy.'

We move on to deal with the question of finding a Captain. That, and watch leaders 'coming up too fast'. Reeder begins to press him. 'Is it not a fact you were operating in breach of the Exemption Certificate, that according to regulations your First Mate had to be on an "approved" list?'

Once again Litchfield is vague, he cannot remember the date he applied to the DfT, '…besides, it would not have been reasonable to cease operations just because I did not have an "exempted" First Mate.'

Reeder ploughs on. 'Was there not some "covering up" and lies told over Orde's certificate?'

Litchfield looks shocked. 'I don't think that was the case.'

'Then let me ask you this, would you deny there was no one on lookout that night?'

'Most certainly I would, because any novice can do that and there were plenty of them on deck.'

I hear Rupert give a long sigh. Reeder continues, 'Yet Mr Minter-Kemp and Bobby Cooper both insist they were short of hands that night, what do you say to that?'

Litchfield looks shocked again. 'That is certainly not true.'

'Then let me ask you this, do you deny that Mr Finlay had never been on a square rigger before and that you were in breach of Load Line regulations, if only by the number of people on board?'

Litchfield concedes, 'Well, maybe that, possibly.'

'And is it right that taking in the forecourse became a matter for debate?'

'What is wrong with that?' he says almost in disbelief.

'Are you seriously suggesting that sail changes are a matter for debate?'

Litchfield realizes he has dropped a clanger, then makes matters worse by trying to cover up by rhapsodizing about Bobby's agility. 'It wasn't a problem, even in that wind, because young Cooper was like a monkey aloft.'

Reeder shakes his head, turns to the Commissioner and the two men exchange a glance. Stone announces an adjournment.

Now anyone who was there that day knows for certain Mark Litchfield is a liar, for all that he has blue blood in his veins.

22

FORGERY
PLYMOUTH, OCTOBER 1985

It is the evening before the day when Robin and Rupert must both cross-examine on the subject of the Captain's licence, something that Rupert regards as the one 'sexy' element in this whole, murky affair. They sit in the deserted restaurant, a bottle of whisky before them, as they discuss this new witness.

'It's someone Bill suggested. We had a job finding anyone, they're not exactly lining up,' says Robin.

'What do you put that down to?'

'Litchfield's "connections" – but you'll be able to tie him in knots.'

'It's not him I'm worried about. It's that bloody woman.'

'The lovely Belinda?'

'Watch her tomorrow, she'll weave some fantasy and Stone will go along with it.'

'But it will all change...' says Robin, '...when Bill comes over.'

Rupert sighs. 'It could still go wrong. We're up against the government, who can do as they please, and the best-laid plans can go wrong.'

Reeder begins the next day's session. 'Mr Litchfield, last night we finished considering the question of manning, and now I want to ask you some questions about events in Antigua and Bermuda. But first let us come to John Adams's letter. If I may refresh your memory I will read out a passage: "It is no good blaming the DfT or any act of God, the plain fact is that there have been continual complaints about delay, late arrivals, late departures, lack of information and incorrect information." Let us begin with the coastguards.'

'No, I am not going to discuss coastguards. It was Mr Massey who brought all that up. We were not breaking any English law.'

Reeder counts to ten, turns over a piece of paper and says, 'Then let us take ventilation. In complaints made by crew, would it be true to say that this was something you had not addressed?'

'Not really, I do think about it every now and then.'

The Commissioner weighs in, 'Mr Litchfield, if I may refer you to a statement you made, that a knockdown was an acceptable risk, is that really your case?'

'Well, it depends...'

'Let us say your centre-line hatches are underwater, is that an acceptable risk?'

Litchfield starts to prevaricate and Reeder interrupts: 'Is it not a fact that you treated the questions of rig and stability in an "ad hoc" fashion?'

Litchfield denies this so they turn to 'radio weather transmissions' and to why the crew were paying no heed that night, and what exactly their orders had been.

It is a relief when Stone says, 'Who goes next?' and Admiral McKinney is announced.

'Sir,' begins Rupert, 'if you could look at the licence you have just been shown, can you tell us if that is anything like a licence you have ever seen before?'

'The format is common but this is not one for an ocean-going vessel,' says McKinney.

'The part that reads "Upon the waters of the Atlantic Ocean"? Would that put you on enquiry?'

The Admiral shifts uneasily. 'I would be inclined to suggest you ask a US Coastguard about that.'

'Did you say you knew of Captain Finlay during the period 1976 to 1980?'

'Yes.'

'You met him again in 1977, is that not right?'

'Yes, sailing the Caribbean.'

'What I am coming to is this. We have the self-same boat described as "being in restricted waters from 1976 to 1980". Can you help me on that?'

'They were moving between summer chartering on Maine waters and went to New England for winter chartering, that is what I would say,' the Admiral clarifies.

'Would it perhaps be that they were talking about two entirely different periods, because on page 85 we have a statement by somebody, stating that Captain Finlay served on that boat in a limited geographical area?'

The Commissioner leans forward. 'Would that be between June and September 1978?'

'Indeed, sir,' replies Rupert, 'yet on Captain Finlay's curriculum vitae we have a much wider period indicated for the same boat, so I wonder if you can help us as to why there might be that inconsistency?'

But the witness cannot do this and Stone looks grim. 'Unfortunately the person concerned is no longer among us to answer to this. But you have made your point squarely, Mr Massey.'

Rupert bites his lip. Will it make any difference to the end result? He can almost hear Thatcher saying, 'Look, the man is dead and you have had your orders, Litchfield must be cleared. Any other outcome will reflect on the Secretary of State.'

Robin must now examine Litchfield. Rupert is hoping for fireworks and offers up a prayer that in a few months' time his witness will be Commander William Peterson, US Navy, in person. But before Robin can begin, Bucknall introduces a diversion: to lay the ghost of the Captain's forged licence, Bucknall has decided it was not necessarily a forgery and that there is another possible explanation.

'Really?' says Stone.

'Sir, I believe I can prove this.'

She goes on to suggest that on the day Captain Finlay's certificate was prepared, the typist involved had broken off her engagement and to revive her spirits, she took a cup of coffee to her workstation and inadvertently spilled coffee onto the freshly typed document. Fearing the office manager would chide her, the young woman may have used some Tip-Ex to correct this, and suggests therefore it cannot be called a forgery.

'Sir,' she says, 'there is another matter I feel should be dealt with today. Mr Cecil-Wright was informed by Mr Reeder that if he was going to make an allegation of fraud against Mr Litchfield, he must have independent proof material in his hands. Mr Cecil-Wright's answer, as I noted, was this: "Mark was a character who would find forgery an acceptable way out of a minor problem."'

Then she goes in for the kill. 'Sir, it seems to me that plain as the nose on your face such material is inadequate to support a charge of fraud and I would respectfully invite this court to order it be withdrawn from the record.'

The Commissioner sighs. Her story is preposterous but the words have been spoken. 'I think,' he begins, 'as those words are now on record and have been heard by all, even if it is deleted from the transcript, the issue is live until I hear from Mr Massey.'

Perry gets up. 'Sir, I apologize for bringing this to the court's notice but I venture to say I think it should be made clear, if people are going to make allegations which take up court time and possibly damage someone's reputation in another place, that person must bear the cost. Sir, that is the only observation I would wish to make at this stage.'

Stone says tightly, 'I am not going to make any ruling but have already mentioned costs and the power of the court and invite everyone here to act responsibly.'

23

LITCHFIELD'S 'CROSS'
PLYMOUTH, OCTOBER 1985

'Have you got all the clippings?'

Rupert is on edge. Any minute now he must come face to face with Litchfield: it has all been about this moment and the nerves are getting to him. He pats a pocket, takes out his pipe, tamps the tobacco, then forgets to light it. He is an odd man but fights for Ben as if his heart is in it, and it cannot be easy to stand against a regiment. For they are all out to get him, even Stone, who, for a while seemed on his side. Downstairs they will be rustling paper, sharpening pencils, getting the acid out. There is no way this will be a clean fight.

'Chop-chop,' says Rupert. I pick up a pen, notebook and a sheaf of papers. Time to go down.

In the courtroom, the copytaker sits alert. As for Belinda, her face is a mask and you must have been trained at Bletchley Park to decipher the expression on Reeder's face.

Of the two protagonists, Litchfield looks defiant, Rupert, less the suave lawyer than wily gypsy.

'Mr Litchfield, I have some questions to put to you on behalf of the mother of Ben Bryant. First, can I ask whether you consider yourself to be an honest person?'

'My own opinion is that I am.'

'Are you law-abiding?

'On the whole.'

'What does that mean?'

'That I occasionally drive cars rather fast.'

'Did you ever crash a racing car?'

'Most drivers eventually do.'

'Have you ever been out in a dinghy that capsized?'

'Probably.'

'Then let us turn to your career in the Navy. Would you say that it was on the whole successful?'

'Yes.'

'Were you promoted?'

'You cannot be promoted in peace time, not until you have served eight years.'

'So you left before being promoted, is that what you are saying?'

'No, you are saying it not me.'

'Would it be true to say your time in the Navy was free of incident. Were you ever admonished?'

'I forget...once or twice. Maybe.'

'Mr Litchfield, why did you leave the Navy?'

'Because I wanted to.'

'So you were not cashiered?'

'I have answered the question.'

Rupert holds the licence aloft. 'Turning to the question of the Captain's licence, can I ask you if this is a copy…or a copy of a copy…of the Master's licence as you saw it then?'

'I suppose it is a copy.'

'At some stage I would like to see the original. Did you read it in detail?'

'I suppose that I did.'

'And Captain Finlay, do you suppose he would know what kind of licence he had applied for?'

'You are asking me to go into the mind of someone no longer with us.'

'You needed a Captain urgently and were prepared to break the law for the sake of financial consideration, would that be fair?'

'On this single occasion, yes.'

'Do you recall seeing the words "waters of the Atlantic Ocean" on the licence?'

'I do not remember.'

'You knew his licence did not entitle Mr Finlay to sail offshore, yet were quite prepared to break the law. That is what your answer amounts to. Did you, personally, copy the document?'

'Probably not.'

'But the document was not a US Coastguards Licence, was it, Mr Litchfield? Can I also ask if you took copies or altered the document in any way?'

'No.'

'Yet someone in your office did.'

Litchfield does not reply.

'Would you agree that you used Captain Finlay illegally for three months?'

'I was overstepping regulations, yes.'

'I am not going to accept that as an answer.'

'Yes, he was acting illegally.'

'He was? It is a fact, is it not, the licence was changed using Tip-Ex or some such substance?'

'I don't know. Maybe the US Coastguards got in a muddle.'

'Is that a serious answer?'

'Very serious. I have a right to make a helpful suggestion.'

'Earlier I asked if you were prepared to break the law for a financial consideration?'

'On this single occasion, yes.'

'Which is to say you were prepared to break the law for the sake of money in a matter concerned with safety.'

'I don't see what it had to do with safety.'

'But it was a breach of the law?'

'Yes.'

'And are you seriously saying obedience to law is a matter of discretion?'

'Sometimes.' Then he adds tightly, 'Are you asking me if I altered that document, Mr Massey?'

'Yes I am.'

'I am not going to answer yes or no. I will have to start again if you want me to answer the question.'

'We will move on, shall we?'

The Commissioner coughs. 'Mr Massey, you have taken things as far as you can with this witness.'

'Sir, he knew Captain Finlay and we have the document. All I am trying to do is to put the two together.'

'But I do not think that you can put that to the witness.'

'But it was a breach of the law?'

'Yes, it was.'

Stone interrupts, 'So you cannot take this any further with this witness. If you want to make an allegation you can, but on the evidence so far I shall refuse it.'

'Then I shall not bother to make it.' Rupert changes tack. 'Mr Litchfield, you have been at pains to point to the many thousands of pounds you spent on *Marques*, so can I now ask whether you have put in all the bills that apply?'

Litchfield 'supposes' that he did but was abroad at the time.

'So where are the invoices?'

Stone comes in. 'Why do we need invoices if the work was done?'

'Because, sir, we have evidence the work was badly done and I am suggesting we should examine them, that the court does, and that it is relevant to see what was spent.'

Stone mutters about 'wasted costs'.

'Sir, I am trying...' says Rupert, '...to establish how much was spent on *Marques* and can only account so far for £12,000.'

Litchfield bursts out, 'I did not come to this court prepared to answer questions like that.'

Rupert rounds on him. 'But you must have come prepared to be criticized for the fact you misled the DfT. Have you not read newspapers since the ship went down, noted public concern? I want to know how you arrive at the figure of £100,000 and suggest that it was a misrepresentation to your MP...a lie.'

Stone's face is red. 'You cannot use words like "lie" to the witness!'

'Sir, I do so because of the pusillanimous manner in which the Secretary of State conducted examination of this witness, I feel obliged.'

'You may feel obliged but in my opinion are not,' says Stone, ruffled. Then he says, 'Where do we go now? E124, did you say, Mr Reeder?'

Reeder rises. ' Sir, I consider it necessary to educate Mr Massey on the duty of counsel to the Secretary of State because of his total ignorance of my position and his outburst, tinged as it was with gratuitous insult. This Inquiry has been conducted with the utmost impartiality.'

Rupert stands his ground. 'Can I pause there? I find it extremely distasteful to have to make these accusations and had the Department of State done its job I would not have had to make them. I would rather not be in this court, I would far rather my client was not a party to these proceedings but having come to this court and seen the manner in which things are conducted, I feel obliged to do so.'

'You may feel obliged but in my opinion you are not,' says Stone once again grimly.

24

THE SHOWDOWN
PLYMOUTH, OCTOBER 1985

We are upstairs: the room is silent except for the scratching of Rupert's pen.

I am standing at the window watching the seagulls wheel through the sky. Up there it is a different universe. The words of a poem Ben wrote at fifteen run through my head. He had called it 'a poem with no title':

They have all gone now but the waves
Still form: the trees still sway
The guns still smoulder.
There is no element of destruction,
Such as us, the humans.
Peace and tranquility. Where is the destruction we need so badly?
Stereotypes must change
The Lions and the non-pacific humans have battled
It out, the blood still flows from the freshly dead.

Whose turn is it to be the Baddies? Perhaps the Birds
Should try or maybe they are too weak or too stupid?
I know: do away with the destructive element!
Now listen, the philosophers tell us, we need the destructive
element
Or the world is not the world.
Stereotypes will have to change.

There is something I want Rupert to do but I don't know how to ask. It has been running through my head all day. Sitting in court, listening to Litchfield, it became ever more urgent. The sense of outrage I had felt at learning of Ben's death over the radio has not lessened. All these weeks I have sat and listened: marked up transcripts, kept my head down and my opinions to myself. But now I want my moment. I want to know, through Rupert, why Litchfield never contacted me. I want him in common decency to say, 'Yes, Ben was lost on my ship and I am sorry for your loss.' Ben cannot speak for himself so, as his mother, I must ask for him.

Outside, clouds have begun to gather and the smell of rain is in the air. Rupert's pen ceases to scratch. I hear him put the cap back on the fountain pen. Any moment we must go down: it is now or never.

'Rupert, can I ask you something?'

'Not now.'

'I need you to ask him a question.'

He brandishes the briefcase, 'What do you think I'm going to do?'

'I want you to ask him why he didn't write to me.'

First, he stares. Then his nostrils dilate. He looks like a bull about to charge. 'I've got to pin something on the bastard, something causative,' he spits the word out, 'something he did, that could have killed nineteen people.

'This inquiry is about why that vessel sank in less than two minutes, but you want me to ask the bloody man why he didn't write you a letter… They are all down there with the knives out, waiting to cut the ground from under my feet. And you want a letter of condolence! We need to focus on what's at stake here.'

He takes out a handkerchief, mops his brow. I ought to shut up. Instead I say, 'I thought it would show him for what he is.'

'They don't care! Don't you get it? I don't care! It's totally irrelevant. Only one thing matters today, what sank that ship! This is a Public Inquiry.'

In court Anthea mouths, 'What's wrong?' I shake my head and under my breath say, 'Ben, help us, please, be here.'

Everything is a fog at first but finally comes into focus.

Reeder is on his feet. 'Sir, I wish to educate Mr Massey on the duty of counsel to the Secretary of State. His total ignorance of my position, and his outburst, tinged as it was with gratuitous insult, ignores the facts. Every attempt has been made to conduct these proceeding with strict impartiality.'

Rupert, now past caring, spits out, 'Impartiality! Mr Reeder asked Mr Litchfield one question about the certificate.

One. To me, that seemed wholly inadequate. When I began here I made a reference to the dubious background of this case and the fact the Secretary of State is responsible for a Department which could be found at fault. Sir, it seems to me only natural justice that Mr Reeder should be seen to be pursuing these matters with vigour.'

Stone says, 'I do not think you are called upon to make these comments, or that it is in any way critical that those acting for the Department for Transport have not seen fit to take the matter of the alleged forgery any further.'

'Then Sir, I will pursue this no further. But ordinary people, those I represent, will want to consider if justice has been served.'

Stone's face is unreadable. Then, in neutral tones, he says, 'Shall we resume?'

Rupert turns to Litchfield. 'Mr Litchfield, earlier we were examining your experience of sailing. Can I now ask if you are au fait with the phrase "tacking and wearing"?'

'Are you trying to imply I am some sort of novice?'

'You are on record as saying the ship foundered, not from any earthly reason, but an "act of God". That was your view, was it not?'

'Yes, and it remains my view.'

'But the facts do not bear that out. I put it to you, in view of what has come to light, that statement is, to say the least, inaccurate.'

Stone will not allow this. 'That is as good as saying he is lying.'

Rupert lets rip. 'Self-evidently, Mr Litchfield is being both inaccurate and evasive. I have been examining him since eleven o'clock this morning, putting to him areas of fact where he was inaccurate. One has only to look at the transcript, where on at least 130 occasions he said that he 'could not remember' or 'does not recall' or 'might have done' and I would respectfully suggest that this is a prima facie case of the witness being evasive.'

'And I am saying you cannot take this any further,' says Stone.

'Are you saying I cannot ask questions about opportunity and motive?'

'You can, but on the evidence you have produced so far, I shall refuse it.'

'Then I will pursue this no further. But ordinary people, those I represent, will want to consider if justice has been served. For, should it be decided to review this Inquiry at some future date, the cost to the Public will be at issue.'

'I do not think,' says Stone, 'that you are called upon to make those sorts of comments about the way matters are being conducted or that it is in any way critical that the Department for Transport have not seen fit to take the forgery further. I will hear you in submissions. I thought Mr Reeder put boldly to the witness that he was acting contrary to what the certificate demanded, in the area of "frames" and so forth.'

'Sir, there was a foul-up with the anchor, crew were tired because they were up late.'

Litchfield interrupts, 'That is not relevant, they would have got at least five hours' sleep.'

'With respect…' – Rupert rounds on him – '…there is not much you do think is relevant to the accident, is there?'

Rupert weighs up the idea of throwing his papers in the air and storming out. Then he remembers our row upstairs and puts a hand out. I realize that, with nowhere to go, he has decided he may as well go for broke. Turning to Litchfield, he asks, almost casually, if Ben was insured. Litchfield falls over himself to explain that crew were urged to take out their own insurance and sign a form agreeing to this.

Now, Rupert, like a magician offers the very form that Ben signed. He holds it aloft and reads it aloud to the court. Under 'sex', Ben had written 'Yes, please' in his crabby hand. A bubble of laughter erupts. Ben, the child of two actors, pleased at getting his laugh, has materialised beside me and giggles in my ear.

As for Rupert, he has become a panther and is stalking his prey through the long grass. He asks indifferently, as if it scarcely matters, 'And when the ship foundered, Mr Litchfield, did you take any steps to contact the mother of this particular deceased?'

A hush falls as everyone waits for his answer.

Litchfield is now the rabbit caught in the glare of the car's headlights. There is nowhere to go. You can almost hear his brain working, as he begins to obfuscate. 'Mr Massey, that was the subject of a very long letter…a letter that probably took a few days to research...produce...set out...fully and exactly...and is very, very complicated... with timings and so on.'

Rupert does not say what have timings got to do with it, but takes another tack. 'Did you at any time send a letter of condolence, or information or a telephone call, or anything at all to Ms Cooklin to tell her that her son had died, yes or no?'

'A letter of condolence...' Litchfield repeats the words as if he has never quite found the time to address his mind to the matter. 'I think there was letter...of condolence...but I cannot be absolutely sure.'

Rupert is implacable. 'Did you sign it?'

'I would have thought that I would have done...I cannot remember...I would have to look through my files to tell you.'

'Did it not occur to you, Mr Litchfield, as a matter of human decency, that this was something you ought to have done?'

Now, no matter how many lawyers he has, he stands alone. No one, not even Belinda Bucknall, with all the might of Lloyd's of London behind her, can help him.

'No, in the context of the time, no it did not.'

You could have heard the proverbial pin drop.

25

COWBOYS AND INDIANS
PLYMOUTH, OCTOBER 1985

'Well…' says Robin, '…that was some "cross".'

'Did you plan to go into all that stuff?' John asks.

Rupert shakes his head. 'No, but they boxed me in. I had to do something.'

'Well, I think it was bloody marvellous. Waiter!' John calls.

'Actually, it was my fault,' I say.

'Really?'

'Yes.'

John laughs. 'You slay me, you two, you really do! You're alike in some ways. Perhaps you should have read law, Shirley.'

'I almost did,' I say smugly.

'Oh?'

'But it was not law I was after yesterday, it was justice.'

'Ah, the blind lady,' sighs John.

Rupert shakes his head. 'No, it was my own decision.'

'Really?'

'Napoleon said, "Listen to advice from all but only act on one's own plans."'

'Never mind all that,' John says, 'what we all need now is a drink. Where's the waiter…oh, there he is, a bottle of Merlot if you please.'

We were on our second bottle when Robin put his napkin down. 'I say we do it and do it now.'

'Do what, Robin?'

'What Stone won't do, investigate the forgery.'

Everyone looks at him.

John says, 'What exactly are you suggesting?'

'That we enlist a local plod.'

'A what?'

'A policeman, you idiot.'

'Go over Stone's head?'

'The wine's gone to your head,' says John, 'and we haven't even opened the second bottle.'

'Actually…' – Rupert is thoughtful – '…it might be a good idea.'

'Really?'

'As citizens we're entitled to ask the police to investigate a crime.'

Straight after lunch Robin takes off for the police station. Rupert goes to reception to ask if they can spare us a room and comes back rubbing his hands. 'We can have the room adjoining the Inquiry.'

'You do realize there's only a wooden partition,' warns John.

'So?'

'Litchfield's girlfriend will have her ear pressed to it. Racing certainty.'

'That's a chance we'll have to take. It's the only room available.'

Looking back, it seems off-the-wall. We assembled and waited for Robin to return with Constable Hellier. He is a fresh-faced Cornishman and asks, 'Can you give me some background.'

'A Public Inquiry is taking place in this hotel concerning an accident at sea.'

Constable Hellier gets out his notebook. 'Details, please.'

'An "incident" in which nineteen people lost their lives,' says Rupert.

'And this was where?'

'Bermuda. Over a year ago, during the Tall Ships Race.'

'When exactly?

'Third of June 1983.'

'Day...night?'

'Three in the morning...Captain's below, crew short-handed, a few raw recruits who'd just joined, chaos...'

Rupert warms to his theme, paraphrases, tells the story in bullet points, for at any moment someone could put a head round the door.

'And the background?'

'Ship's owner was a mean bugger, didn't want to put his hand in his pocket, engaged a Captain who would work for free, and this is where the forgery comes in. When the ship went down, the owner was in dead trouble. It has been established that someone forged the Captain's certificate either before or, more likely, after his demise.'

'So,' says Detective Constable Hellier, 'where is this forged document now?'

Everyone looks at Rupert. 'On my desk in the court.'

'Can I see it?'

Rupert says, 'If Shirley would be kind enough to go next door, it's on my desk...'

'It's OK,' I say, 'I know where it is.'

'Wait...' says Constable Hellier. 'We must preserve its integrity. Can you put it in an envelope?'

'Sure, I'll get one from reception.'

'Hold it by your fingertips at the corner.'

I enter the court, trying to look inconspicuous, and sidle up to Rupert's desk. All eyes are on Litchfield, who is being cross-examined by Beattie. 'Perhaps you could tell us why, presented with a document, prepared by a professional surveyor, you did not act on his recommendations?'

'I suppose...' Litchfield says sulkily, '...I did not regard it as very important.'

'That will not do, will it, Mr Litchfield? I put it to you that you ought to have known it was.'

Sliding the document into the envelope, I make myself scarce and then Detective Constable Hellier goes off with his spoils, leaving us giggling like schoolgirls.

Next day is Friday. Rupert leaves early but I stay on to take notes, in case anything comes up. Next week I shall be working on a 'soap' and Rupert has another case.

I am just about to leave when someone mentions the forged certificate so I sit again. Perry is on his feet, trying to remedy the damage done by counsel for the beleaguered surveyors. He asks Litchfield, 'Did you ever discuss with Captain Finlay what qualification the DfT might require?'

'No, I don't think so.'

'To put it another way, did you give him the impression, however unwittingly, that if he did happen to alter the certificate, no one would ever know or care?

'No,' says Litchfield, but suddenly realizes Perry has given him a 'get out of jail free' card and falls over himself to say of course if the Captain had altered the certificate it is more likely he did it earlier. 'Aha!' says Perry. 'Now we're getting somewhere.'

Being a Friday night, the Commissioner decides to call it a day. As everyone is putting papers into briefcases, Perry pipes up.

'Sir, where is the Captain's certificate?'

The Commissioner, his mind on his whisky and soda, says carelessly, 'It is somewhere about, I imagine.'

Reeder says, 'No, sir, it does not appear to be.' The room goes quiet.

'Well, where is it? Nobody would remove it without asking, surely?'

I try to look nonchalant.

Perry says anxiously, 'I hope it has not been taken to another authority', and mutters like the White Rabbit in *Alice in Wonderland*. The Commissioner goes red in the face. 'Is there a chance it could be in Mr Massey's room?'

'If so it is behind a locked door...' says Reeder grimly, '...and it is my understanding Mr Massey does not intend to be here for some days.'

Perry says excitedly, 'We could force the door, sir?'

The Commissioner huffs and puffs but shakes his head. 'I am loath to go down that route. Does anyone know when he is expected back?'

I mime picking a piece of paper up from the floor.

'Mr Reeder,' says the Commissioner, 'take the first opportunity of asking Mr Massey where it is.'

I scribble a note asking Robin to keep an eye on things while I'm away and to please let me know if the document is mentioned again. Then I rush to catch my train.

On the Monday evening, Robin rings. 'There was quite a kerfuffle but no one mentioned breaking the door down again. Stone got red in the face and said if other counsel want a court exhibit, they must apply in open court and he wanted the document back, and soon.'

On Wednesday, Robin rings again. It seems we are to resume in London in the New Year. Also, Reeder brought up the subject of the missing document again.

'Did they say any more about breaking Rupert's door down?'

'No, but Reeder reminded Stone the problem was not resolved.'

'How did he take it?'

'Huffed and puffed but decided to wait for Rupert to arrive. I think he's worried about a bill for damage.'

On the following Friday in the courtroom, there is no sign of Rupert. It is getting on for three o'clock when the door opens and Rupert flies in and goes straight to whisper to Gross. He nods and then says, 'Sir, I was about to resume with Mr Longbottom but Mr Massey has something to say.'

Rupert bows. 'Sir, I am grateful to my learned friend. On the matter of the document of Captain Finlay's certification, I have made further enquiries.'

As an actor, I know that Rupert is playing his 'Third Act' and nudge Robin in the ribs.

'Sir,' says Rupert, 'I am asked to say that a letter of reference is needed from you to the Chief Constable, if you wish the police to investigate. The procedure is simple. I am asked to say that it must be done in writing. A formal letter by you to the Chief Constable or a gentleman called Detective Inspector Booth, will be followed by an interview at which Inspector Booth will take a statement.'

Into a stunned silence the Commissioner speaks. 'Which is equivalent to saying you suspect a crime and have invited the police to investigate?'

'Exactly, sir.'

'Thank you for that information,' says Stone, through gritted teeth.

Rupert goes on. 'It is of course my client's position that she wishes the matter to be referred by the court.'

I clutch Robin's arm as the Commissioner controls himself with difficulty.

'I think, after that, we will leave it to the Treasury Solicitor to keep parties informed.'

26

THE DEPARTMENT FOR TRANSPORT
PLYMOUTH, NOVEMBER 1985

Finally, it is the turn of the Department for Transport to be examined. With Rupert in London I was on my own. I wanted to hear for myself how they could justify what happened. Ben too, was curious. 'I want to see the bastards' faces,' he said. Stone gave me an odd look when he saw me sitting there, beside Ben – though he could not see him – as Ben said conversationally, 'Where's Rupert Bear?'

'London.'

'Better fish to fry?'

'He's only contracted for a limited number of days. I'm lucky to have him at all.'

'You're good at persuasion, Mum.'

'Nice to be good at something.'

'Don't fish.'

'I want to see their faces, hear them say the words.'

'They did what Big Brother told them...' says my very own anarchist. 'It's the capitalist system, I told you.'

'Shush, they're going to start.'

'Who's that bloke with the white hair?'

But Mr Darlow is speaking. 'I am a principal Ship Surveyor in the Cardiff Office of the Department for Transport.' He has blue eyes, laughter lines, looks a typical seaman and seems pleased with himself.

Reeder begins, 'You first met *Marques* in 1982. Where would that have been?'

'It was in Bristol one summer evening. I had gone with a party from a wine circle and was walking along the quay when I noticed an old galleon and wondered whether to go aboard. As a Board of Trade Surveyor, I can. And then I thought, no, you are with friends and it is a summer evening. But something about the vessel intrigued me. So next day I got in touch with Captain Martinez, suggesting he have a look at her. On receiving his report, I sent the file down to London and then, so to speak, it left my sphere of influence.'

Reeder asks, 'Your next contact was in November of 1982 when Captain Martinez told you the vessel had returned to Bristol. Can I ask why you were chasing up *Marques*?'

'Purely for my own curiosity. I knew the ship had to be kept under observation, but we would not do the normal survey on such a vessel. I took the view that a person telling you they have done this, that and the other, is all very well but if there is a bit of proof, if you have seen what they paid for and what materials they used, then you have something to go on. It is not good policy to hide away large sections of your ship behind difficult structures. And when it comes to a wooden ship, any wooden ship, the greatest dangers will come from fire, wrecks or a capsize. I chatted to the owner, a Mr Litchfield, who said, "I have already done a lot of the things you mention, last year in Spain, and I can prove this by showing you a photo."'

'Did you tell him what the DfT would require?'

'Oh yes, I said we'd want a survey. Neither I, nor any other Board of Trade Inspector can issue a certificate on the strength of someone else seeing it. It's like a policeman who finds your Road Tax is out of date, he'll look at your tyres and so on and if it's an old banger he'll pull you to pieces before he is finished.'

'Do you ever rely on photos?'

Darlow shakes his head. 'They won't tell you if the next plank should have been taken off too. I would have fired the information down to headquarters for the Stability Department to pick up the bones of it and see what they think.'

'So when you are considering "hatches", would it be true to say that you are looking for something pretty watertight?'

'Well, let me put it this way…my front door will let the wind in if I do not shut it.'

Darlow is called back to the stand. 'Had you ever come across a proposal like that before from Head Office?' asks Reeder.

'Never. When I joined the Royal Institute of Naval Architects, we had Associates, who were not necessarily professional in the industry. I once knew a man who sold ship's carpets who was an Associate.'

'Would it be true to say that at the meeting at the DfT, you were the only one who had inspected the ship?'

Darlow agrees. 'Yes, but a ship's keel is a ship's keel and frames are frames. You can look at a thousand photos and see planks have been removed but you cannot tell if that was all that was necessary, or if the next plank ought to have come out. You leave that to the integrity of the surveyor. This is why I said at the beginning we would have to open the ship up again. Only the man who has seen for himself, can say if the ship is right and sign the declaration. I said it at the time and say it again, if Litchfield's man was accepted then he took over responsibility. There is no way...no way in the world you can survey a ship a thousand miles away from her dry dock, not with all the photos in the world. I had no idea they were going to accept this man Perryman. We have never before had an outside surveyor or done a survey retrospectively...' He pauses. 'Don't get me wrong. I accept that it was perfectly legal, it has just never happened before and once I found headquarters were thinking along those lines, that they had changed the rules, as it were...quite legally...I did not attend the meeting as a stability expert...I just happened to be there and I am only reporting to you what I remember as one of three people at that meeting...' – he pauses again – '...accepting that Perryman was a policy decision taken at a level above me.'

It is not cold, but I shiver. No one would believe that lives had been put at stake. I want to know more; I am finding this stuff hard to believe. Checking the list for the next day, I find that it will be the man who approached the Minister with an unlawful proposal suggesting they do Litchfield a favour: this I cannot miss.

'I had been a Minister in the DfT for a few months,' he says, 'when I received a letter from Andrew Rowe, Member for East Kent, about a letter from a constituent...'

Looking at his long thin face, I think, this is the man who sent my son to his death.

'...the letter was from a ship owner who faced red tape at the DfT.'

He waffles on about 'the hardships' of being a minister: how it was difficult to remember something which had happened two years ago and he spoke of Litchfield's letter, in which he mentioned a Mr Perryman, with a string of initials after his name. He had no idea what they stood for but assumed his officials would know.

Reeder says, 'It might be said the Department were being put under political pressure. What would you say to that?'

'That I consider it part of an MP's job to be helpful to the general public.'

'And would you be kept informed?'

'Not necessarily. It's usually a case of "on to the next meeting".'

'In that case,' says Reeder jovially, 'I shall sit down and it will be "on to the next counsel".'

And that was it, the sum total of Reeder's probing. I kept reminding myself that, God willing, Ben's legacy would be that the guilty would be punished. There is still time.

Kay stands. 'Do you understand that inspections of vessels may lead to Certificates or Exemptions being issued? That people rely on them? You had been in the job a month. Were you aware of the seriousness of what you were doing?'

Stone is terse. 'I have only two questions for you. Firstly, were your surveyors influenced in any way by the fact this ship was to be used for sail training? And secondly, did that lead to a reference that this matter needed to be approached with extreme caution?'

The next witness is Mr Noble.

'Did you have any doubt about the legal position?' asks the Commissioner.

'I was not sure what to think, to be honest. Mr Holstead told me he'd had a letter from a Mr Litchfield about the treatment accorded to his vessels and was saying that he intended to go and see the Minister.'

'And what was your reaction?'

'I might have said, "What sort of game is this?" You try to please the Minister but I was not there so I can't say if he was put under any pressure. An "Associate" can be anyone on the periphery of shipping matters; a pump manufacturer might be an Associate.'

And then Gross says, 'Had you read the *Marques* file by this meeting? Were you aware there was no stability data on board? Because my question is why did the Department effectively ignore the stability requirement for *Marques*?'

'I don't think we ignored it,' says Noble nervously. 'I don't deal with stability. I am in charge of load lines... Stability is a different section...people don't mention stability to me...not in the normal way.'

On the third day the examination of Noble and another DfT surveyor, Mr Holstead, continues.

'I was doing my job,' Noble insists. 'I explained in my statement that the whole idea was to accept Perryman's survey in lieu of a Department survey. I was backed up an alley, so to speak.'

He waffles on, telling a story of how he had toadied up to a Junior Minister, so wet behind the ears that it never occurred to him that by doing a 'favour' he might be condemning people to death.

'Stability, did we deal with it properly? Well, if you mean it in accordance with the requirements of the 1968 Load Line Rules, no, but then we were not applying the Load Line Rules.'

Gross: 'Did you ever say to Mr Holstead, wait a minute, we haven't got any hydrostatic data? I come back to the same question I put to you yesterday. The Department failed to deal properly with the entire problem of stability for *Marques*. It is blindingly obvious that you yourself were wholly influenced by instructions from above.'

'Not wholly influenced,' says Noble, in a small voice.

'Substantially influenced, then?'

'No. Instructions came from above to examine Mr Perryman with a view to accepting his surveys.'

'Thank you,' says Gross.

The Commissioner says, 'Help me with this, Mr Holstead. Do you think it satisfactory to discuss a letter from an MP with the Minister when you were not fully conversant with the Department's files on the ship? Twice at least the Department had recommended that the Load Line Certificate was needed for this particular vessel.'

Holstead is defensive. 'I did say that to obtain the Load Line it was necessary for the vessel to be surveyed by DfT surveyors.'

'You told the Minister that, did you?'

'Yes.'

'You are quite sure about that?'

'Positive.'

'You did tell him that it was very unusual?'

'Yes.'

'I ask, because you may have been present when the Minister said he does not have any such recollection. Tell the court in your own words exactly what the Minister said to you.'

'The problem was I knew nothing about this chap and the Minister said, "Look, have you never interviewed anyone for a job? Take him out for a drink, have a chat and if he comes up to scratch, consider accepting his survey."'

'Did you voice any reluctance to the Minister?'

'No.'

'You didn't probe this report with him at all?'

'No.'

Reeder reads out, 'The declaration needs to be completed by Mr Perryman. This is necessary in case of casualty to show the responsibilities of Perryman and Litchfield,' and then asks, 'Tell me this, was the object to get the DfT off the hook for not doing its job properly in case of casualty?'

Holstead says miserably, 'I had the benefit of Mr Litchfield, the owner, who had spent money on the vessel, because the Department wanted to make the certificate valid for two years but Perryman would only sign for twelve months. They agreed to have a further meeting in October, only Perryman could not be there.'

Reeder: 'So the vessel was not opened out then? It makes me wonder how carefully you probed what had been done.'

'I felt Perryman was competent.'

'If you were asked, Mr Holstead, to go down that road again, would you do it?'

'In my position I have got to be open to approaches, which are not strictly in accordance with the rules. And I felt that the vessel had an adequate degree of stability. I am certain that the maritime world as a whole is looking to us for the future...'

When he saw the transcript later, Rupert wrote, 'God help us!'

An article appeared in the *Times* the next day under the following headline: 'STORM STILL BLOWS OVER REAL LIFE DRAMA BEHIND SINKING OF MARQUES'.

To millions of television viewers, she was the Beagle charting treacherous seas to enable Charles Darwin to unravel the mysteries of evolution. To others she became the rugged heroine of The Onedin Line *but when she died during a savage squall off Bermuda with a loss of nineteen lives she bore her real name:* Marques.

Yesterday, the Inquiry into the loss ended in Plymouth after eight stormy weeks but the ordeal has been merely postponed and will begin again in London in April, when it must determine whether the ship, which looked so grand, was a leaky old tub. Relatives have heard already that before the final tragedy Marques *had nearly sunk three times.*

In the function room of a hotel, a saga as salty and controversial as any fictional plot has been unfolding. Allegations of incompetence, revelations of forgery, tales of sabotage have all been recorded. Witnesses have not even agreed on the stability or condition of the 72-year-old 85-ton vessel, which sailed from Bermuda to Halifax, Nova Scotia, in July last year. One carpenter, Mr Tom Gavin, who took part in a refit in Spain, said her condition was a 'running joke' but another carpenter claims her timbers were 'in good condition' and according to Mr Rupert Massey, acting for one of the victims, 'gross and reckless errors' contributed to the disaster.

Four Britons were among the dead. Mr Peter Messer-Bennetts, of Wadebridge, Cornwall; Mr Benjamin Bryant, aged 18, of Kentish Town, London; Miss Gillian Shaughnessy, aged 24, of Chelsea; and Mr Ian Brims, aged 48, a father of three from Hove, East Sussex. Already one American lawyer has filed a claim for $55 million. Other lawyers wait in the wings to seek damages from the American and British Sail Training Associations. One alleges that the addition of a third mast and poop deck for her Beagle role made her unstable. The atmosphere has not been helped by the animosity between Mr Robin Cecil-Wright, former co-owner, and Mr Mark Litchfield, who legally became sole owner of Marques. Even during the Inquiry, the two men continued their legal battle. It has been established that Mr Stuart Finlay, aged 42, captain of Marques, who died in the disaster with his wife and young son, had used a forged certificate. Only the inquiry can decide whether Marques should have sunk but how she did is clear and it happened soon after she left Bermuda on the afternoon of July 2, buffeting gently into a four to six wind.

PART THREE

WHITEWASH

27

SIX MONTHS LATER
LONDON, APRIL 1986

Half awake, eyes closed, I wonder where I am.

As the cats start to scratch at the door, I remember that I am back home in Grafton Road. The confusion is due to the fact that after a six-month hiatus, the Inquiry has reconvened. We are in London now at a place in Westminster called Church House. The first day was all about Rupert's examination of Lord Napier. It should have been his big moment but his feathers were ruffled by Jervis Kay. He accused Lord Napier of being a landlubber and Rupert was absolutely furious. But on the whole, I am feeling optimistic as Bill is due to arrive, this time invited by the Commissioner. He writes that he's bringing a friend called Dwayne D. Fitzgerald, who sounds straight out of a movie '...but he's an Attorney...' writes Bill, '...and we all call him Buzz. By the way, he is looking forward to meeting you.' For insurance, Bill is bringing a colleague, Roger Long, to speak to the evidence. He fears, being related to a deceased, that they could accuse him of bias and he's taking no chances.

Closing the front door to leave the cats to their own devices, I set off down the road to the newsagents. I'm hoping for a reference to Rupert's examination of Lord Napier and want a copy for the file. Standing in the queue, all I can glean is that the *Guardian* piece looks short and the front-page headline in the *Times* is PEER APPALLED AT CHAOS, so buy both.

I'm standing at the bus stop, newspapers under my arm, and a woman smiles as if she knows me. The press are all over the story, so maybe she recognizes me. Side by side on the bus, she reads over my shoulder and remarks chattily, 'I thought I recognised you. It's Ben's mum, isn't it?' That's what they call me. 'Dreadful case, I wish you all the luck in the world.' At the Co-op in Camden Town, she gets off. I take out the letter which came today:

Dear Shirley Cooklin, My wife and I thank you for your letter of 24th March. In September 1980, we were expecting our son's return from Japan, when we heard over the radio, his ship, the Derbyshire, was 'missing at sea'. I served 43 years in the marine industry. From the DfT we got stalling and I am convinced of a government cover-up. You are to be congratulated for getting an inquiry and I should very much like to meet you. Yours sincerely, Peter Ridyard.

This letter was not my only or first connection to the *Derbyshire*. Back in 1984, I wrote a piece in the *Observer* headed THE TERROR OF LOST AT SEA. I received a shoal of letters, some from women who had lost a child. One of these women was called Vivien King, whose son was lost on the *Derbyshire*. We met for lunch at a pub in Islington, shared reminiscences, laughed and cried. Today's letter seems more than mere coincidence. A pattern is emerging: we are not alone in encountering resistance from the DfT.

As the bus heads for Whitehall and we swing round Trafalgar Square, I anticipate the day ahead. Awaiting the arrival of the Americans, we are marking time. Meanwhile, Reeder and Stone have climbed on the bandwagon and stability is now the hot topic. I must be on my toes as Rupert is bound to be in a foul mood after yesterday.

Outside Westminster Abbey I get off. Six months ago, in Plymouth, Rupert threatened an apoplectic Stone with taking the forgery to New Scotland Yard, and now we are just around the corner. Church House is an august building, opened by Queen Victoria in 1883 to be used for clerical matters. These days it houses conferences but still has the aura of religiosity. In fact, just across the road, I noticed yesterday a shop selling religious regalia. As a Jewish child, accustomed to clergy in sober black, I would have been astonished. Today, as a non-observant adult, I still find it strange to see vestments and religious regalia on sale like apples and pears. I don't quite know why, but maybe it has to do with the feeling, that in this establishment of Church and State, pretty well anything can be bought and sold.

I pass through the grand portals into a hall with a shiny marble floor and a great deal of oak. This place was built to inspire awe. It succeeds. Choosing between an elaborate oak staircase and a lift, I opt for the latter, noting a pendulous light fitting in iron and glass and a noticeboard barded with flyers and announcements. We expect to be here some weeks, and as the lift ascends, I attempt to get some sense of the place. Speculating on Rupert's mood, if yesterday is anything to go by, he will still be seething over Jervis Kay's examination of Lord Napier. Rupert regards the peer as his property and it has not escaped my notice he is keeping us apart. Emerging from the lift, I see him standing outside the courtroom and to judge by his expression, he is still not over yesterday.

He grunts at me. 'Weather is on the agenda again today and Shearman still on the stand. Kindly collect quotes for future reference.'

'Surely, once Bill and Roger arrive, it will all be about stability?'

'We can't afford to put all our eggs in one basket. Besides, I don't trust Reeder.' Next he says some reporter from the *Guardian* is on his way, whom I am to take to lunch.

'Where? There are no restaurants round here.'

'There's one on the ground floor.'

So, it's first downstairs to book a table then back up to take my seat. In court they are still knee-deep in weather. Still, it makes a change from Yacht Club Admirals. By twelve we are back with stability, and they go on and on about 'Mr Crone's curve'. It's a relief to head to the lobby to meet Gareth Parry. I am surprised to find that the restaurant reminds me of an up-market Lyons Corner House. As a child, in the days before the Yanks came, I was taken there for a treat. The waitresses, too, look not unlike the Nippies at the Corner House, while the atmosphere is heavily clerical, with dog collars everywhere.

'So,' says Gareth Parry, 'what went on in Plymouth that took eight weeks in court and here you all are again?'

'There was a lot of hostility.'

'Are we talking lawyers or witnesses?'

'Both...'

He frowns.

'...key witnesses were kept away.'

'Kept away by whom?'

'Either the DfT or Litchfield, which pretty much came to the same thing.'

'What are you implying?'

'I'm not implying, I'm saying that it was rigged.'

'That's a serious allegation. Are you accusing the Commissioner...'

'No, Stone was straight, but key witnesses were kept away.'

'Who, in your view, was behind this?'

'For a start, you have to understand that Litchfield and the DfT are in bed together.' I explained how Thatcher's hand was forced. He smiled when I told him about Lord Napier. He said he'd always regarded him as 'an old buffer'. Thinking I must entertain him, I go on about 'spying' in bushes, writs being served and how one local scribe got the wrong end of the stick. Government lawyers were apoplectic after a banner headline 'Barrister alleges gross and reckless errors' appeared.

'Sounds livelier than most Public Inquiries I've covered.'

'And when we got the police in...' I roll my eyes.

He starts to laugh. 'Who is "we"?'

'My brief, Rupert Massey, myself, Litchfield's ex-partner, Robin Cecil-Wright, and the writer John Goldsmith. We called in the local police about the forgery.'

He laughed. 'Not sure how much of this I can use, but do carry on.'

'Rupert said I was to give you a flavour. The real meat is about to begin.'

'Good,' said Parry. 'Then let's get something to drink. I don't usually when I'm working but this is starting to sound like a good story.'

After lunch, in court they went on about local weather with an expert called Shearman, who said 'the squall phenomenon' should have been mentioned. Later, I told Rupert I had made sure the *Guardian* would be there when Roger and Bill arrived.

Next day, Finlay's certificate came up again. 'Mr Massey,' says Reeder, 'will no doubt want to conduct an examination.'

I hiss to Rupert, 'What about him?' as Reeder goes on about 'Mr Crone's curve'. Then it was back to stability again, with Perry on his feet being verbose as usual.

'I can tell the court that, on the Wednesday following the casualty, Mr Crone came to ask me if I could reproduce her M lines, as none were available. But hydrostatic particulars will give you displacement and at various draughts also give you the KG, the distance of a Metacentre about the keel, the KM, the angle of the heel and the general characteristics of the ship. This will enable you to calculate the GZ curves and establish the stability of the ship in any conditions.'

He looks round the court as if expecting a round of applause. Everyone is getting in on the act now. Reeder says, 'In the case of *The Eye of the Wind* there was a stability book, which pointed to care on the part of the Master, care that was lacking when it came to *Marques*.'

The Commissioner asks, 'What's the yardstick to warn the Master the vessel has only moderate dynamical reserve?'

'Only that it appears at the top end of the curve.'

'There was quite a debate about that, as I remember, between Dr Baxter and Mr Holstead...' Perry suggests it is not quite so straightforward, '...bearing in mind there is a difference between winds and gusts.'

'Your view, Mr Perry?' asks the Commissioner. 'Would it be right to say, if as in this case, you are dealing with an existing ship, you might consider it unsuitable? Can we have your view on that?'

'Well, yes, I suppose so, if...'

Stone leans forward. 'If what?'

'Well, if you cannot attain the 90 degrees.'

Beattie comes in now like a mother hen. 'I really must protest. Mr Perry is unrehearsed and this is grossly unfair!'

Stone won't have this. 'It is not the least bit unfair. On the contrary it has been extremely useful.'

Reeder jumps up again. 'Can anyone tell us if there is an international standard?'

'All I can tell you is this,' says Perry. 'It is very important, crucial even, that the Master understands the limitations of his vessel.'

'So, can I ask if one factor might be the manner in which the boat is handled?' asks Rupert.

Everyone looks at Perry. 'Yes, that is the top and bottom of it.'

By Thursday, with everyone aware that the Americans are about to arrive, a Mr Harvey, a senior figure in the DfT, is wheeled in to pronounce on what is now the burning issue.

Reeder asks whether *Marques* should have had stability information on board.

Harvey looks uncomfortable. 'Yes. Strictly speaking.'

'So should *Marques*'s stability be described as good, excellent or awful? *The Eye of the Wind* was "Moderate".'

Harvey replies they have been in contact with Woodin and Marean and the US Coastguards. He understands Roger Long will be here next week. He says brightly, 'But we have worked out how our sailing ships comply with the US regulations and I could have these printed, if the court would like that.'

The Commissioner says the answer to that is 'Yes' and Reeder puts his oar in by saying they might need a debate about whether these sorts of ships should even be considered for sail training.

Rupert asks, 'Can anyone tell me exactly why *Marques* was not required to carry stability information?'

'It was required,' says Harvey, 'but having been converted from sail cargo to sail training, made it unique.'

'Then if *Marques* was obliged to carry such information, why was it not required to satisfy a stability test?'

Harvey looks at his feet. 'I think you should ask other people that.'

Rupert insists, 'Can I ask him, as a senior organ of this Department, if everything was laid out in regulations, why was such information not forthcoming in respect of this boat?'

Kay says, 'The original purpose of rules and certificates was to stop unscrupulous owners from running "coffin ships" across the Atlantic?'

Harvey wonders why these idiots cannot understand. 'Even this M notice I am producing, I must convince Ministers they are necessary or be met with a cry of "Next thing you'll find UK ships disappearing off the flag!"'

On Friday, Collins, a naval architect, takes the stand and Harvey is recalled. Gross asks Collins, 'If the hatch had been on the centre line, can you estimate the difference this might have made?'

'Probably another minute or maybe a little longer,' he says reluctantly.

Then Rupert asks Reeder the only salient question. 'Can you tell the court this, in the light of what we heard yesterday and today, does the Secretary of State intend to extend the Questions, or make any amendments?'

Reeder says grandly, 'I do not envisage anything to take anybody by surprise. Nothing has emerged which inclines us to conclude that anybody is guilty of causative fault.'

The Commissioner looks relieved. 'That is exactly what we would expect to hear.'

'I do not intend,' says Reeder, 'to make the sort of speech one sometimes gets from the Secretary of State and give reasons as to why it was alleged...'

Rupert's eyes meet mine. As to the forgery, he will take instructions.

Stone decides to ignore the fact they debated this six months ago and Reeder promises to have answers by next hearing. Stone suggests it would not be helpful to have the answer after we have dispersed. Perhaps Reeder could see where it was going?

At this moment, the arrival of Long and Peterson is announced.

'As it is Friday afternoon,' says Stone, 'and in the light of today's evidence, I wish to study one of the bundles and suggest we should now adjourn.'

Rupert and I lock eyes. At last we will be in the driving seat. But will the arrival of the Americans prove the panacea we hope? Or will the government, as Rupert seems to think, find a way to 'weasel out' at the eleventh hour? That is the sixty-four-thousand-dollar question and, as Rupert never tires of saying, we must beware of hubris.

28

THE AMERICANS
LONDON, LATER THE SAME DAY

Fleet Street on a Friday night. The pub is packed but the door keeps opening, as yet another bedraggled figure staggers in. London is living up to its reputation. Outside it is cats and dogs; in here, it's like a Turkish bath. Seeing an empty chair, I sit. Rupert, looking distracted, is in his usual state – somewhere between anxiety and doom. Everything hangs on the success of this partnership.

Peter, busy entertaining Roger and Bill, has just rounded off a funny story when a transatlantic voice says, 'Penny for 'em, Shirley'. Buzz, or Duane D. Fitzgerald, is beside me. 'No causative fault? They've got to be kidding.'

'What do you think of it all, Buzz?' I ask.

'What I can't get my head round, is that the regulatory body should behave in this way,' he says.

'They do it because they can get away with it.'

'Nineteen lives...' he says. 'This is not some third world state.'

'Let me tell you something, a vessel called *The Eye of the Wind* was in the same case as *Marques*, needed a load line, did not want to pay. What do you suppose happened?'

He shook his head. 'I'm no good at riddles.'

'The DfT did it for free.'

'But that's good news, no?'

'Not if you know the reason.'

'Which was?'

'Prince Charles was their sponsor.'

'What are you saying?'

'That who you are is what counts here. I got this Inquiry by sheer luck.'

'Correction. Luck and persistence. My money's on you, kid.'

'OK. Persistence and a lot of luck.'

'Hey, I don't accept that.'

'It's the hypocrisy I can't stand. It's so bloody...English.'

'You should come to America,' says Buzz.

'I nearly did go. Once.'

'Come and visit with us.'

'Maybe when this is all over.'

'We must celebrate,' says Buzz. 'If only to cement Anglo-American relations. I am going to take you guys out to dinner. I'll give my wife a ring and tell her to join us.'

I asked Buzz if we could include Peter 'For sure. Hey, let me tell you my take on all this. Karen Davidson said you

were immediately open to helping American families. Had you two not engaged, they might have got away with it.'
He shakes his head. 'I have to say, kid, your conduct was distinctly un-English, in my experience.'

'That's because I am only second generation and Jewish to boot. My granny hailed from Nishny Novgorod.'

He laughed. 'I knew there had to be something. I said to Bill, that girl is no Limey.'

'Ben would have expected me to make a fuss. He knew I was a terrier.'

'Don't compare yourself to a dawg, Shirley, let's go for Joan of Arc.'

'Alright, a cog, Buzz, a facilitator. Had you known Ben...'

'Kid, I know you. He was your son and that's all I need to know...' He looks at his watch. 'We will get there, no question, because we are talking crime, we are talking manslaughter and there is only one way for any right-thinking person to go. But enough serious talk, let me buy you a drink before we go eat, this is supposed to be a celebration. What'll it be?'

'A gin and tonic, please, Buzz.'

'And I had you down for a whisky sour. How wrong can you get?'

Monday 14 April. First there is an anti-climax, as Reeder has decided that first Mr Crone must speak about the work he had done. Bill and I exchange a glance. Eight weeks in Plymouth, where the only person to mention 'stability' was Rupert, suddenly everyone wants to get in on the act.

'May it please you, sir,' begins Reeder, 'it would seem proper, before hearing the American evidence, to call Mr Crone, from the Department, to speak to the work he has done.'

I whispered to Rupert, 'Why are they doing this now?'

'Mr Crone…' intones Reeder, 'could you tell the court your responsibilities in the Department?'

Crone looks uncomfortable. 'I was primarily involved in casualty investigation.'

'Would it be right to say that something else ought to have been done, or that the event which took place ought to have been anticipated?'

'No one can predict everything. Things happen fast at sea. *Marques* had only one mast. But a greater range of stability would have been desirable.'

'I put it to you, Mr Crone, the Department knew very well that an inclining experiment told you little about the stability characteristics of a vessel, is that not true?'

Crone crumbles. 'I suppose so.'

'So whoever made or authorised modifications, gave insufficient attention to the safety characteristics of this vessel?'

'The Spanish data was not available.'

Rupert gets up. 'Oh, I am sure it was but we should have to look at whether it was revealed.' He strikes an attitude.

'Does there not seem something strange to you, when for one hundred years they have had Wright's *Principles of Naval Architecture* to help them?'

One almost felt sorry for Crone, who was now carrying the can for the entire Department. But his agony was not over, for Rupert made a final attack. 'I put it to the court that this witness has told us his report is independent but I am suggesting to you that it is not.'

Perry rises. 'Sir, counsel is bullying the witness.'

Rupert says angrily, 'I submit that I am entitled to examine him. A great deal, a very great deal of information, was raised by Department surveyors, of which he makes no reference. This includes the down-flooding angle of a fully loaded vessel, as it affects the condition of the companionway hatch. It would help my clients if measurements could be provided.'

He goes on to speak wildly of calling new witnesses and even recalling Litchfield. His counsel says that his clients would have the strongest possible objection to that and a row looks on the cards. Commissioner Stone reminds everyone, 'Our American witnesses have come a long way and perhaps this was the moment to proceed.'

Then, finally, Roger Long gets up to take the oath. 'I, Roger Long, do solemnly swear...'

Roger looks so young and earnest as he adjusts the big easel and checks his graphs. He is with us 100 per cent. We are in a different room today, one with a high, sloping ceiling. The quality of light which comes through those tall windows has a feeling of wind and sea. There has been no sighting of Ben recently but I can sense his spirit. And just at the moment Roger signals that he is ready to start, the sun comes out from behind the clouds and floods the room with light. Never mind hubris, I think, because surely the gods are with us. Now, Roger takes up a position besides his easel. What was now apparent was the very real concern about the vessel. We had centred on 'stability' and 'management' and were edging towards a level of 'carelessness' that could mean the difference between life and death. Perry's fury at the mere idea of recalling Litchfield tells us we are now in dangerous waters.

Reeder asks Roger, 'Can you tell us the exact implications of US regulations?'

'We aim,' says Roger, 'to prevent the loss of a vessel by capsizing.'

Everyone knew that *Marques* had 'sailed down' and did not capsize.

Roger begins, 'The foundation of modern safety stability analysis was laid down in the late 1800s by Sir W. H. White, the Chief Constructor for the British Royal Navy. He wrote the famous *Manual of Naval Architecture*, which is now the acknowledged and primary source for methods used by United States Coastguards to evaluate sailing stability.'

'I see,' says Reeder. 'So there would be no "exemptions" in the US, is that what you are saying?'

'None, sir,' says Roger .'The vessel's range of stability was so low that by the time the water began to enter the hull she had lost the ability to right herself.'

There was a long silence. It was left to the Commissioner to say, 'Well, in the light of that statement…' – he turns to Reeder – '…how do you suggest we proceed, Mr Reeder?'

'Might I suggest, sir, the court consider these documents overnight? I realize this may depend on the court's commitments.'

Stone says wryly, 'It may also depend on the court's understanding!'

That evening we gathered again in Rupert's Chambers.

'So, what do you think?' I ask Bill.

'They can't ignore the evidence.'

Rupert shakes his head. 'It's a good start but let's not get excited. Let's wait and see what they come back with.' He looks at me. 'There has still been no word of the forgery.'

'But this is the standard for the US Navy,' says Bill. 'I would be surprised if it were not for Britain's Navy too. How they can go against that?'

'Who knows? They may just be holding their fire, we must at all costs…' – I chime in and we say together – '… beware of hubris.'

Roger looks astonished but Bill shakes his head. 'You British…' and we all laugh.

Next morning begins with a red herring, which is par for the course in this Inquiry. They were waiting to see if Roger would consolidate his case – surely it could not be all that cut and dried? But the day begins with an argument on an entirely different matter.

'Mr Reeder,' the Commissioner asks, matter of fact. 'What news do you have on the forged licence?'

'I don't know, sir.' Rupert puts on a show of surprise. 'But I can make enquiries,' Reeder replies airily.

'That would certainly be a good idea.'

Rupert rises. 'I must protest, sir. Six months ago Mr Reeder volunteered to look into this matter, and promised to bring the evidence to court.'

Stone says irritably, 'He has just said he is going to do it now.'

'But we have lost six months, and sir, I must protest, this information could and should have been before us today. It was discussed at the end of the last recess and I have the strongest possible objection to the way this has been handled, and hereby give notice that I intend to deal with it in my final submission.'

'You can make your objections in that way if you wish, Mr Massey, that was not what I intended. We can look at the transcript later and...' – his voice rises – '...we are.'

'But this is eight weeks later!'

Bill's face is unreadable.

'Sir,' says Roger, 'I would like to explain to the court how and why we conducted our comparative study.'

The Commissioner leans forward. Detail was what he liked: evidence he could see and touch. Here was a man with a mathematical bent. 'I should like to see *The Eye of the Wind* on a graph at some time,' says Stone.

Roger refers to his graphs. 'I refer you to numbers twenty-two, twenty-three, twenty-four minus and twenty-four. You will see that this unfortunate ship, *Marques*, was a vessel of unusual characteristics – shared by vessels in this study, also capsized by wind forces.'

He pauses to take a sip of water. 'All sailors have confidence and pride in their vessels, including many with a high casualty rate. But, sir, we are not saying they sail out of the harbour, turn left and fall over; what we are saying is that eventually circumstances catch up with them and casualties are highly likely. Almost by definition a sail training crew, any you care to name, is deficient. The clue is in the age of the participants. With children or youths, a high value is placed on their lives. Therefore, every sail training ship needs a high degree of stability. Sir, this vessel needed very close looking at, very close indeed.'

Rupert gets up. 'Is it your view this is something that should have been obvious to any reasonably competent naval architect?'

'Yes, sir. Let me try and show you why the "lines" appear similar but the conclusions differ.' He draws a graph, then stands back. 'I believe that will give you some idea.'

Reeder gives Stone a look. 'Sir, I should like to direct you to page 19 of the transcript from Day 33. This fully justifies the conclusion we both came to in our earlier discussion.'

Rupert, furious at being excluded, comes in. 'It is all very well, throwing these things in, but scarcely equitable unless I have a right of reply. If it please the court I intend to deal with the matter of the forged document at the end as I do not have the Transcripts in court.'

Stone is happy with that. They are in the middle of complex evidence and he, for one, needs to concentrate.

Now Roger returns to his blackboard to explain his theory pictorially by drawing his curve. 'This is how White himself explains it...' – everyone tries to understand – '...this is a very dangerous vessel, very dangerous indeed. Had I been asked to cast an eye over the ship, I would have said at once that it was unsuitable, merely by inspection of the righting arm curves. To make myself clear, I am saying, even without any comparison, merely by looking at the relationship between the deck edge to the peak of the righting arm curves, that vessel should never have been used for sail training, and what is more...'

Rupert interrupts. 'I am sorry to labour the point, but do the safety characteristics of the vessel go to the line and suddenly decline, so we have a sharp division between the vessel on one side or is there a curve of some kind to be drawn?'

'I shall have to use the blackboard again,' says Roger.

Maths has never been my strong point and by now I had ceased to follow. Roger seizes the chalk and begins to draw again. 'As it declines on this graph the probability of disaster becomes higher and eventually the probability catches up with the vessel. Or, if you move down the graph, it becomes much more dangerous...' He extends the line. 'However, if the vessel can withstand this wind velocity, then there is a very good chance she is going to capsize.'

'So, what you are saying is that *Marques* was the most dangerous vessel in the world of this kind?' asks Rupert.

'That we know of.'

The court shuffles. People try to avoid looking at each other. I thought I had spied Ben. Not jokey Ben, the one who used to make his schoolmasters quake. Certainly this one looked like an avenging angel.

Jervis Kay rises. He begins to cross-examine Roger with a sneer. 'I think I am right in saying, Mr Long, you told Mr Massey you would have expected a naval architect to decide this vessel was unsafe on sight.'

Roger replies calmly, 'I believe scepticism is very important. For as doctors fight disease so do naval architects fight the loss of vessels. Scepticism, in both cases, is one of the best weapons in their arsenal.'

'So, you are saying, are you, that he ought to have retained a naval architect?'

Roger turns to Beattie. 'I don't place too much credence on survivors' reports; these survivors believed their vessel was safe.'

Reeder comes in. 'So, is it your evidence a naval architect should take no notice of how she sailed but study stability data?'

'Yes, that naval architect should not have recommended that vessel for sail training. It is hard for me to believe nobody took that first step or asked that first question, which might have prevented this tragedy.'

That night none of us had the energy to go out. Tomorrow would be Bill's turn and after that we hoped it would be over. Ben did not appear again. Maybe he too was beginning to feel that enough was enough.

Next day we went over the same ground again. Roger was re-examined and he repeated what he had already said. When Rupert asked him, 'Would it be true to say your evidence is that no level of warning would have assisted the Master under those conditions?' he answered, 'Yes,' then he paused. 'Always assuming she had sailed.'

Now Bill takes the stand. Reeder asks, 'Can I ask if you have any formal qualifications in naval architecture?'

Bill answers wearily, 'Yes, from Miami University.'

'How did you become involved in this Inquiry?'

Bill speaks of hearing news reports on TV and radio, then learning his sister had been on board. Trying to get information from the DfT or Litchfield. 'Following that,' he said, 'I did preliminary calculations and was amazed this vessel was even at sea.'

'Let us suppose you knew the owner, would you urge him to exercise extreme caution when sailing this vessel offshore?'

'Absolutely.'

'You would give a specific warning, would you, of each unsatisfactory feature?'

'Most certainly, that is my area of expertise. I teach stability and trim now for the Navy.'

Rupert rises. 'Commander Peterson, I would like to ask you some questions regarding the late Captain Finlay. Supposedly, he was a trained quartermaster and navigator. Would you expect him to know something about stability and trim? Would he be likely to avert to safety warnings in a stability booklet?'

'I cannot imagine otherwise.'

'I have here a copy of his licence...' – he motions to the clerk – '...perhaps this could be conveyed to Commander Peterson. We know that Captain Finlay had very limited experience of square rig.'

Then Kay is on his feet. 'I put it to you, Commander Peterson, that your late sister, Mrs Susan Howell, never showed concern over this vessel.'

Bill's voice is cold. 'Perhaps you would like to pursue the matter with my sister. I would have to rely on hearsay but can tell you she called her husband and was very concerned indeed, about both the rig and the large, open hatches.'

'So, why didn't she mention this to Vice Admiral Weschler, who was on the judging panel for the race?'

'It is entirely possible that she did.'

Kay tries again. Those of us who were at Plymouth remember Gillespie's 'changed statement' and the pressure put on survivors to adhere to Litchfield's 'script', and now he says, sanctimoniously, 'We, here in this court, can only go on the evidence before us.'

'My information is different,' says Bill curtly. 'I am just repeating what I was told. My sister believed the vessel to have been properly reviewed. That is all I can tell you.'

The Commissioner steps in. 'I am not sure where this is going, Mr Kay. Commander Peterson came to help us. You have put what Mr Gillespie said to this Tribunal. As to anything else, I do not honestly see where this witness can help us any further.'

Next, Beattie tries to rubbish Bill. 'Let me ask you this, Commander Peterson. I would hazard that you do not go to the dentist unless you have toothache, would that be right?'

'Oh yes, I do, sir,' says Bill. 'I go twice a year to get my teeth cleaned.'

There is a spontaneous burst of laughter. I did not laugh. I was too angry at the way Bill was being treated.

Then the Commissioner, with his habitual courtesy, says, 'Commander Peterson, let me say at once, on behalf of the court, how grateful we are to you for coming to assist this Inquiry, and I would like, if I may, to go through some of the points you make. Let us suppose you had been consulted in 1983. What would you have advised the owner?'

'I would have told him the danger of loss of life is in direct ratio to the amount of time a vessel can stay afloat. Some vessels have few casualties because they have a full five minutes, which can be a long time in such a situation. But warnings are not enough. Events at sea happen fast and often a warning might not get to the man at the helm or the Captain below, and what we do know, sir, is that in this case the Captain did die.'

There was a long silence.

Reeder rises. 'Sir, it must be apparent to the court, and everyone here, that we have been moving in the wrong direction. If the views of Mr Long and Commander Peterson are accepted, then in 1982 or 1983 a competent naval architect would have condemned *Marques* as unsafe. I feel bound to say that I see no reason to apologize for changing my mind at this late stage. Lawyers must always seek guidance from experts and follow professional advice, especially where this supersedes empirical evidence, so "causative fault" is not only arguable now but a very strong case indeed, and this makes an analysis into the vessel's history necessary. Therefore we must review the situation, as regards Mr Litchfield and Mr Perryman, we have no other option.'

Stone nods. 'We are of your mind, Mr Reeder. I shall need to consider Mr Perryman's position and send him a letter, as a matter of urgency.'

Rupert jumps up. 'Sir, until today I was the only party suggesting causative criticism, and the opposition this engendered was substantial. My client's sole interest in this case was to ensure the right questions were asked. She did not take a view. All this is in the Transcripts, Commander Peterson was my witness, Mr Long was my witness...'

Stone interrupts. 'Mr Massey, if one could spell things out before we began there would not be much worth in having an Inquiry. I expect things to alter. At the end of the day all that matters is that the truth emerge.'

But Rupert has not finished. 'Would Mr Reeder not agree that Mr Peterson was originally our witness?'

Reeder says, through gritted teeth, 'I accept that Mr Massey kindly initiated the Peterson inquiries. This will, no doubt, be kept in mind when "costs" applications are made.'

Buzz whispers, 'Sounds like you've done it, kids, let's head to the nearest hostelry and raise our glasses to victory.'

Rupert hears this and I see his face change. Buzz is saying he is taking us all out to dinner. He will call his wife, and where can we find the best oysters in London? We are all in a state of euphoria; all, that is, except Rupert. Yet in the midst of celebration I feel a pang as I think of Ben, and remember that none of this will bring him back.

In the taxi, Roger does an impression of Reeder. 'This has been blindingly obvious, guys...' and we fall about. After dinner Buzz raps on a glass. 'Guys, your attention, please. A toast to Shirley, who made herself such a thorn in the side of this government...and of course to Rupert,' he adds diplomatically.

'Hear, hear!'

Rupert says, 'We are not there yet. I don't trust Reeder and never have.'

'Oh come on...' Buzz chides. 'The poor girl has worked hard for this moment, as have you.'

Bill says, 'I'll raise my glass to that.'

'Reeder pretends to go along with this because Stone is enthusiastic, but take it from me, he has his own agenda, and let us not forget that Reeder represents the Secretary of State...' – Rupert pauses – '...and ultimately the Prime Minister.' He shakes his head. 'This thing is by no means over.'

Buzz puts on his 'attorney's hat' to quiz Rupert about what might happen next. He replies that the court will be busy with Perryman and he did not intend to be there for that. Buzz raises an eyebrow. Later, when we find ourselves alone, I explain that I am not paying him.

'So who is?' asks Buzz.

'The *Sunday Times*.'

Buzz insists on hearing the whole story and I tell him how I rang the editor to ask if they would fund me. Buzz says, 'Anytime you want to cross the water, Shirley, you can join my firm. You're a breath of fresh air.'

Later, more seriously, he asks what 'strokes' they might yet try to pull. Rupert says the government can do as it likes: Reeder is 'the mouthpiece' of the Secretary of State and as such has enormous power.

'Yeah, I've got the picture,' says Buzz. 'Stone is nominally Top Dawg, but the real power lies with Reeder.'

I insisted it was Nicholas Ridley in person who was guilty. It was he who had instructed officials to 'relax the rules'. For my money he should be in the dock.

Buzz shakes his head. 'This is all crazy.'

29

AN EVENING AT JOHN'S
LONDON, APRIL 1986

At the end of April, the court stood down.

It's late morning at Church House. We are sitting over coffee in the restaurant as Rupert posits a 'brainstorming' with Robin and John, in order to work on the 'Final Summation'.

That morning I had received a letter from Peter Roberts, Managing Editor of the *Sunday Times*:

Dear Shirley,

Just a line, somewhat belatedly, to thank you for your kind note of April 1st on The Marques Inquiry. I do hope that justice will be done, though nothing can undo the tragedy of that sad affair.

I know that you said Mick Brown was keeping an eye on the inquiry from a story point of view: I hope he is still doing so and that if you hear anything newsworthy you will let him know.

With best wishes

Yours sincerely

Peter Roberts (Managing Editor)

There was also a letter from Buzz: Fitzgerald, Conley & Haley, Attorneys at Law in Bath, Maine:

Dear Shirley,

I truly enjoyed our work together in London, and I look forward to hearing of positive results. It is very obvious to me that the inquiry would not have occurred had it not been for your persuasive efforts.

I have written to Rupert requesting copies of the transcripts of the Questions and Final Summations. I hope that he will send them to me soon. I am not certain as to whether I will be travelling to London in May, but be assured that I shall not set foot in the UK without contacting you.

Please extend to Peter my warmest best wishes and thanks for the several pints he bought me.

Warmest regards

Sincerely

And above the typed signature, Duane D. Fitzgerald, he had scrawled 'Buzz'.

A week later we all gather at John and Anthea's. There, replete after a splendid supper, the four of us – John, Robin, Rupert and I – go upstairs to John's office, eager to toss ideas about, like a salad, as the photocopier hums away in the background. Rupert, at the head of the table, rifles through notes. 'The trouble with this case is where to begin.' He runs a hand through his hair.

John says, a gleam in his eye, 'Why not start there?'

Rupert looks up. 'Sorry?'

'Well, the others were all after something. They had had an axe to grind...' John ticks off on his fingers: 'the DfT were hanging on to their jobs, Litchfield was trying to hide the truth, Belinda Bucknall was a mouthpiece for Lloyd's...'

Rupert cuts in. 'You've left out Jervis Kay and I don't know where he fits into this scenario, do you?'

'Ah,' John says, 'the Sail Training Association is a bit of a bummer. Logically speaking, they were impartial but had an axe to grind like everyone else.'

'For my money,' says Robin, 'they were for keeping the old salts quiet. But you are right, they were partial. So maybe that's your opening: everyone was partial, except for you two who spoke up for the dead.'

Rupert bangs on the table. 'Then that's our opening,' he starts to declaim. 'The evidence that has been presented to this court, has all been partial, with one exception...etcetera, etcetera, etcetera...' Then, with rather less élan, he says, 'Now all we have to do is write the rest.'

John makes a move to lift the decanter. 'Probably the moment for another whisky.'

Something is worrying me. We are on the winning side, and in theory have the wind at our back. For with those magic words 'causative proof' everything has changed. But has it? A Minister urged his minions to 'forget the rules' and settle things over a meat pie; Ben, out in the Caribbean, boarded a ship only to die on that ocean floor.

Suddenly, I was filled with rage: 'Take him to the pub for a pint and see if he seems a decent chap.' Ye gods!

I cry out, 'I don't see why we've got to hold back: it's not just Litchfield who's guilty. Ridley was elected. Thatcher appointed him Minister of Shipping and the public have a right to expect a Minister to do his job. He is guilty and I don't see why he should not be named.'

There was silence. Trust a woman to throw a bomb. John is the first to speak.

'You do realize what you're suggesting?'

'Yes, but I am right, aren't I, Ridley is the elephant in the room?'

Rupert is coming to a slow boil and says roughly, 'Grow up, Cooklin!'

'Why can't we tell it how it is? Why should a shit like Ridley hide behind his office? He is guilty of manslaughter. It is his job to make laws not break them!'

'And this is a Public Inquiry and not a criminal court...' thunders Rupert, '...and if you think making a barmy suggestion like that is helpful, then you are even madder than I thought. Are you seriously suggesting I should go after the Secretary of State in person...' – he spits out the words – '...because I am the one who will have to stand up and face those bastards and you ask me to commit professional suicide, do you?'

There is a silence like ice. The memory returns of that hotel bedroom, on that day when we prepared to go down and face Litchfield. They were all against him then, even

Stone. Cornered, Rupert had thrown common sense to the winds and pulled it off. He did it because I asked him, even though it was, on the face of it, patently mad. After a pause, I say, 'I am sorry. I am just so sick of compromise. For once I wanted us to speak the whole truth. But you are right.'

'Perhaps,' says Rupert wearily, 'we can now get on.'

30

RUPERT'S 'CLOSING'
LONDON, JUNE 1986

In June the Inquiry kicked off for the last, and one hoped, final time. Perryman was summoned and informed of his rights. Rupert as attacking counsel goes first. Stone gives him a benevolent glance, all disagreements forgotten in a new wave of bonhomie, and Rupert takes the stand to embark on his final address.

'Should the ship ever have left the quayside…'

Can this really be the end I wonder?

'…for if the exemption provisions were intended to waive the survey, then they would swallow the rule and invest the Minister with the power to repeal an Act of Parliament…' Rupert looks at Stone. 'Sir, I urge you to say that the Department for Transport exists to protect people from their own ignorance and folly…' – he takes a long pause – '… Long said, "A sail training vessel is by definition deficient." Lord Napier, a layman, was concerned by the hatches…'

He cases the room, making sure he has his audience. Then he goes in a little harder. 'Sir, in every book on seamanship, one reads, "Do not go to sea, if you are tired" and it is well known that young men think they are invulnerable.'

Stone, head to one side, says reflectively, 'I have a picture of Orde. He stands on the stairs, starboard side, after his watch and does not see over the windward side of the ship.'

Rupert, as if to underline their new entente, follows his lead. 'Yes, and he told this court that a force 11 capsized the boat. Yet to police in Bermuda he said he could not remember the wind strength...' – now he looks the Commissioner in the eye triumphantly – '...and there you have the first of many discrepancies between statements to police and to this court. Sir, we all blame an act of God, when things go wrong. I do not say that the ship was not struck by a squall, but what I do say is this: with young men racing there is an esprit du corps, a feeling that nothing can go wrong. We have all seen it.'

Stone says, 'Thank you for that, it is helpful.'

Rupert had said, over and over, that we must beware of hubris. But as far as I was concerned it was all in the bag and now I just wanted it over. As to what we all believed would be the end of the drama, it was always predictable that he would let me down. Just as he did at the beginning. But I was not prepared for what happened.

I arrived at Church House, ready to play my part as Rupert's assistant, to be met by the Treasury Solicitor. 'Ms

Cooklin, I am the bearer of bad tidings. We have just received a message from Mr Massey. He is not available today, but says you have a copy of his closing speech...' – she gives me a tight smile – '...and trusts you to deliver it. He wishes you good luck.'

For a moment I stood frozen. Was this some practical joke? Then I remembered that government officials don't do jokes. She was right about one thing. I did have a copy of the speech. For a moment I felt unsteady. The Commissioner and his two advisors were seated on a dais, right at the far end. It was a long and very narrow room, rather quaint, with Victorian alcoves and pilasters. Stone and his advisors sat behind these, almost as if they were on a stage. In front of them was a long, polished table. I noticed all this as I tried to stem a rising tide of panic.

Stone smiled at me. 'We are ready for you, Miss Cooklin. Do take your time, there is no rush.'

I began to read out Rupert's speech in a monotone. I was breathing fast and almost too frightened to think. I looked at the sheets of paper but something seemed to have gone wrong with my sight. I managed the first two lines, then everything became a blur. Suddenly I could not decipher it. The words might as well have been in Chinese. Ben was whispering, 'Give it to 'em, Mum, you can do this. Say how hard it has been, let rip!'

Then time played a trick and I was nineteen and standing on a makeshift stage in the Royal Albert Hall: as a first-year student. Stephen Joseph was glaring at me out of those bulbous blue eyes. He was talking about acting, but his words could apply to this situation. 'You silly girl, acting is not about words, it is about being truthful. By the power of your conviction, making others feel what you do.' One might apply this to the current situation. For surely the object of the exercise was to make these fancy lawyers, in their pinstriped suits, realize just how hard and gut-wrenching it had been.

'Sir,' I said, 'you all know I am no lawyer and that I should not have to stand before you today, untrained as I am. For you this is a job but to me it is about my life. My son was eighteen and we are not supposed to survive our children. You have all heard the evidence from America. You know now, beyond peradventure, that boat was unseaworthy.'

I took a very long pause, as I faced them all down (never underestimate the value of a pause). I lifted my head and spoke more confidently. 'So I ask you, all of you, to do your duty as human beings. To find for the innocent and convict the guilty. I know this is not a court of law…' – I faced them down, dared them to look at me – '…but imagine for one moment, your child killed and do as you would be done by.' Then, as if a string had been pulled, my legs gave way and I sat, or fell, into my chair. But I knew it was not over. That somehow or other, I must find the strength to finish and read out Rupert's speech. So, I took a deep breath, filled my diaphragm with air, as if I were going on stage. Then, controlling the tremor in my legs, I stood and read out the speech: the one we had all laboured on that night at John's.

'Sir, my clients faced a cliff-edge of opposition to bring this case to justice but their efforts have been vindicated. What this Inquiry has achieved gives meaning and purpose to what would otherwise be a senseless human tragedy. In that sense, and in that sense alone, can the loss of this boat be called an act of God.'

Then my legs gave way and I sat down shaking like a leaf. It was a great way to end. No one could fault Rupert's gifts as a speechwriter. His downside, as I ought to have known by now, was his unreliability.

Next day the following article appeared in the *Times*, headed 'OFFICIALS ACCUSED ON LOSS OF SHIP', in which David Hearst wrote:

Counsel for the Secretary of State for Transport yesterday accused the department's own officials of making basic errors which led to the sinking of the television sailing ship Marques *in a squall off Bermuda, with the loss of nineteen lives.*

Mr Peter Gross, representing the Transport Secretary, told the public inquiry that Department for Transport officials failed to inform themselves about the true nature of the stability of Marques. *He said, 'It was a basic failure to inform themselves as to the true character of the ship. Without that information there was no true basis for granting the certificate.'*

Arguing against representation from counsel, Mr Gross said that it was not good enough to say that the state of knowledge about the stability of tall ships in 1983, when the certificate was granted, was not sufficient to reach the conclusion that the boat was not seaworthy. The Department for Transport was the regulatory body and in the absence of stability evidence, it relied on the past history of the ship. It was awarded a load line exemption certificate, enabling it to cross the Atlantic and compete in the Tall Ships Race.

Mr Gross said: 'It is one thing to say that you should consider past history. It is an entirely different thing to say that you should rely on past history as a substitution of adequate knowledge of stability.'

In evidence on Friday, Mr Gross said that his clients made no apology for coming to their conclusions 'so late in the day' and added 'but we do say there were, in this case, numerous human errors and although it is much more difficult to say that there were clear breaches of duty, it is the Secretary of State's case that certain breaches were causative....'

He invited the inquiry, held by the wreck commissioner Mr Richard Stone, QC, to find that the co-owner of Marques, Mr Mark Litchfield, failed to inform himself on the stability of the ship after recommendations in an earlier report by a department surveyor and by so doing Mr Litchfield was in clear breach of his duty as the owner.

Turning to the involvement of Mr John Perryman, the surveyor employed by Mr Litchfield, Mr Gross said Mr Perryman had no grounds at all for assessing the ship's stability, other than the experience of Mr Litchfield in sailing her. No line plans were prepared, no work was done on the displacements and sail ratios, all things which according to evidence at the inquiry would have given indications that Marques *was top-heavy.*

Mr Gross said Mr Perryman must be judged against what a reasonably qualified naval architect would have said. He was speaking on the last day of evidence to the inquiry, which has been sitting in Plymouth and London for 62 days. In an earlier internal inquiry, the department had concluded that Marques *was blown over by a squall, that water had entered the sails on the leeward side, and that she sank.*

A week later I had a letter from Buzz.

Dear Shirley,

I was delighted to receive your letter of June 15. Bill called me after talking with you and gave me a rather glowing report on the concluding days of the Inquiry. I was delighted that Gross argued for causative fault, against the Department, as well as Lichtfield and Perryman. In the light of the compelling evidence he had no option.

I await the Decision of the Court but remain confident proceedings were not thwarted by the efforts of Perry, Bucknall, et al. I continue to marvel at your strength and resilience. Please take me at my word and come to the United States for a visit and if you do not come to visit us, Bill and I will be over for the victory celebrations when the Decision of the Court finally issues.

I hope that you know that you have our love and best wishes.

Sincerely

Duane D. Fitzgerald

In the same post there was a letter from Karen Davidson:

Dear Shirley,

I understand that the investigation has finally reached a conclusion, and that you gave a superb closing and received encouraging words from the Wreck Commissioner. Please know that you have my hearty congratulations and appreciation for your hard work on this issue. On this side of the ocean, it appears that the tide may have been turned. I am enclosing a copy of a news article that appeared on the front page of the Sunday paper here. ASTA (the American Sail Training Association) is still maintaining a very harsh posture against my cases, but I believe there is good merit in my arguments against them and am pursuing it fervently.

Best wishes to you.

Very truly yours

Karen Davidson (By Air Mail)

A second letter arrived from Buzz, who had just caught up with the news of Rupert's 'no show' on the last day.

Dear Shirley

I was delighted to receive your letter of June 15, 1986. Bill called me after talking with you a few days ago, and gave me a rather glowing report on the concluding days of the Inquiry.

I am very sorry that Rupert was unable or unwilling to appear for his final speech, but I am confident that you handled the task very ably and, at the end of the day (as you say in Britain), his failure to appear will not change the result.

I, of course, was delighted that Gross argued for causative fault against the Department, as well as against Litchfield and Perryman. He really had little choice in the circumstances, and would have appeared completely ignorant of rather compelling evidence had he not taken that stance.

I shall await the Decision of the Court, but I remain confident that the truth-seeking nature of the proceedings were not thwarted by the efforts of Perry, Bucknall, at al. I continue to marvel at your strength and resilience, and I know that your efforts will protect young people like Ben from the negligence of the Department, Litchfield and the like in the future.

Please take me at my word and come to the United States for a visit. We live in a very pleasant part of the Northeastern US and we would welcome the opportunity to show it to you. If you do not come to visit us, then I can assure you that Bill and I will be over for the victory celebration that must occur when the Decision of the Court issues.

I am dictating this letter on the evening of June 23 as I pack my briefcase for three days in New York. I hope that you know that you have our love and best wishes.

Sincerely

Duane D. Fitzgerald

That letter from Buzz was the final coda. With the Inquiry at an end, and the Commissioner's report not expected for some months, we dispersed. I went to stay with a friend in rural Brittany. In the autumn we would be called to hear Stone's report, then there would be a 'costs' hearing and financial settlements and then, at long last, it would all be over.

31

A FLY IN THE OINTMENT
LONDON, AUTUMN 1986

I had been back from France a few days when the phone rang. It was Rupert. I asked if there was any news.

'If you mean Stone's report, it's too early.'

'Then what are you ringing about?'

He sighed. 'I am rather afraid they are up to something.'

'Stone?'

'No, the Department.'

'But the Inquiry is over. It was over in June. Wasn't it?'

'They don't seem to think so.'

'What do you mean?'

'All I can tell you is that I keep getting letters.'

'Letters about what?'

'I wish I could answer that. I don't know what's going on but Stone wants to see us.'

'If it's not about the report, then what is it about?'

'Your guess is as good as mine. He just says he wants to see us.' Then he added, 'All of us.'

'That sounds ominous.'

'I would not disagree.'

We arranged to meet at Rupert's Chambers. The mild autumn weather had changed overnight and the 'Beast from the East' was upon us. I awoke to find it had snowed in the night. The city lay under a crisp white blanket. When I opened the front door, Violet, Ben's cat, slipped out and went out to explore, her paws sinking into the intriguing white stuff. I decided to leave the car at home and went to dig out my snow boots. Together, we walked in silence across the snowy gardens to Stone's Chambers, which faced the Embankment. I could just see the mast of HMS *Belfast* and recalled when Ben was in Antigua that he wrote to ask his father to go to the *Belfast* to buy him some special knife for splicing rope, an article which, according to Ben, could only be bought on the *Belfast*. The memory of all this brings a sharp pang. Some things never get easier.

Stone's Chambers are dark after the blinding white outside. It was rather like entering a cave. We stamped our feet to get rid of the snow. As I stood inside, waiting, I stood staring at Stone's collection of political cartoons. In all the twists and turns of this strange affair, this seemed the strangest moment of all. What were we here for?

One by one the lawyers sauntered in. First Reeder, then Perry, closely followed by Jervis Kay. It fell to Belinda Bucknall to make the dramatic late entrance. She looked like a character straight out of *Dr Zhivago,* dressed head to foot in black, her hands encased in a black fox muff, her pale, heavy features framed by a black Cossack-style fur hat, which to me looked like a guardsman's bearskin.

Once everyone had arrived we were shown in to Stone's office. He was sitting at his desk, looking bewildered. I knew immediately something serious had happened. Stone was such a calm. orderly man. But not today. He ran his hands through his sparse grey hair, glasses on the end of his nose and said, 'I must tell you all, that I do not know what to do.' Then, spreading his hands, he said, 'Help me, please.'

I sat, as in a dream or nightmare. They talked about some new evidence which had just come to light. We had sat in court for 62 days, spread over a period of three years. One would have thought that everything that could be said, had already been said. But it seemed not. New evidence had come to light, as if a magician had drawn it out of his silk top-hat. It had been lying all that time, in an office drawer at the Department for Transport. Evidence so crucial that it could negate a body of evidence, which had been argued, probed and questioned, for all those months: thirty-six of them.

I let it all roll over me and went home feeling flattened. Then I went upstairs to sit at my desk in the dark. I could just make out the shapes of the pigeons scrabbling outside.

I heard him say, 'It's not your fault, Mum.'

I had wondered when Ben would appear. 'I have let you down.'

'It's not you, it's the fucking capitalist system.'

I had forgotten for the moment that he was an anarchist. 'What's the capitalist system got to do with it?'

He said, loftily, in his businessman mode, 'You wouldn't understand, Mum, and I haven't got time to explain.' It sounded so much like the old Ben that I began to cry. He patted me on the back. It felt like a butterfly's wing.

'Write your play…' he said kindly, as if he were the adult and I the child. 'That will make you feel better.'

'I've finished it.'

'So write another.'

Then there was nothing: just the silence and the snow outside on the roof and the pigeons who looked like the ghosts of real birds.

I thought of the poem he once wrote about birds and I wept.

I had spent three years battling: I had listened to people peddling lies, instead of dealing with my grief, only to find it had all been for nothing. Ben was right, come the revolution.

One day, to unpick evidence that had taken 62 days to amass and ran to thousands of pages? I thought of all those typists, poised over their notebooks: the waste of time, as they took down every word, comma and full stop. And for what? What sort of sick joke was this? I tried to ring Rupert but there was no reply.

As 1986 drew to a close we heard that the Department intended to close things down by producing some uncorroborated new evidence. Bill reacted with grim fury. On 20 February 1987 he sent the following letter to the Treasury Solicitor with a copy to me:

Dear Sirs: re: MARQUES Inquiry

I have reviewed recent Inquiry submissions by the Department for Transport, and the Marine Casualty Investigation Branch, the Wolfson Unit and various parties. In addition, I have studied the independent report by Roger W. Long Marine Architecture, Inc. concerning the Astilleros Tarragons lines. It is my professional opinion that:-

1. The total volume of data regarding stability is adequate and accurate to restate that MARQUES, as rigged at the time of her loss, was exceptionally deficient in stability. It was this which resulted in such a tragic loss. A more 'typical' sailing vessel might have survived such conditions.

There were four more pages of reasoned argument. Bill's style was courteous but beneath it I could sense his fury. He ended with these words:

Seaworthiness is the sufficiency of a vessel in construction, stability, crew and equipment for the service in which it is employed. It is a very grave matter for anyone to conclude, after all the effort expended in this Inquiry, that MARQUES was suitable to be a sail training vessel. In addition to being untrue, such thinking places at risk the lives of the young and inexperienced as well as the future of international sail training.

Sincerely, William M. Peterson

To me Bill wrote:

Dear Shirley,

Thank you for your letter of 13 February, with enclosures. You have been a workhorse on this project and I admire your ability to keep fighting. Enclosed you will find a copy of my comments to the Commission. The real meat of this has been mailed by Roger and I believe his report is definitive on the final lines. I take offense at the way the DfT, Perryman and Litchfield play with the truth, but enough evidence has been presented and it is important to keep the pressure on. MARQUES does not have bad lines, she has the wrong rig. I would be careful not to give Litchfield, et al, any chance to weasel out. Please keep in touch and keep the faith. Roger, Buzz and I send our best to you Rupert, Peter, etc.

In March, Bill wrote to Rupert again, sending me a copy. He said he hoped the letter could be used: that he was still convinced of 'causative fault'. He asked me to make sure that Rupert understood the need to recoup 'costs'. Bill had spent a small fortune in travel to the UK, Roger's and Buzz's fares, hotels and emails and that first trip to the UK 'on spec'. I knew he did not want to tackle Rupert head-on, for fear of rocking the boat, even at this late stage. It left me between the devil and the deep blue sea. The letters ran to four closely typed pages of A4, and began:

Dear Rupert,

It was a pleasure to talk with you on Tuesday and I share your concern over the new position in the Marques Inquiry. Hopefully this letter will be of assistance. I agree that nothing should be taken for granted as we near the end, Roger's analysis was prepared by a naval architect, exactly as he would do for Coastguard Certification, not individuals who claim little knowledge of sailing vessels...

But the real meat of Bill's argument came at the end of the long letter:

...the fact that Marques has no reserve at the casualty condition, means that she is even less safe once a voyage is under way.

He ended his long letter:

Please call if I can be of further assistance and best wishes with your final presentation.

Sincerely, Bill

By March, with uncertainty still rife, I received a postcard from Lord Napier, dated 12 March and posted from St James's Palace.

Dear Miss Cooklin,

I enclose a copy of a letter I had from Lord Brabazon in the Department for Transport, which I thought you might be interested to see. I have written on several occasions to Mr Rupert Massey, but have had no reply, so I can only assume that he is away.

Yours sincerely

Napier and Ettrick

The attached letter, sent from the office of the Under-Secretary of State at the Department for Transport in Marsham Street read:

Dear Nigel,

Further to my letter of 15 January about a further hearing in the Formal Investigation into the loss of MARQUES I can now tell you that the Wreck Commissioner has ordered this to be held at 10am on Monday 23 March in Convocation Hall, Church House, Great Smith Street, Westminster SW1. The hearing is not expected to last for more than one day.

Yours ever (and an indecipherable signature)

There was also a letter from US attorney Karen Davidson:

Dear Shirley

We are still awaiting the report of Wreck Commissioner Stone on the Marques Inquiry. Have you had any news on that? All of my letters have met with no reply and I am curious as to what they are doing [she was not alone]. It is particularly important in the light of the fact that the deadline for filing will expire on June 2 of this year. Please advise if you have any information. I look forward to hearing from you.

Very truly yours

Lovett, Schefrin & Gallogly Ltd.

Karen Davidson.

I awoke next day and switched on the radio, as I had done that day Ben died. Once again, the news had already begun and I heard the announcer say: '...last night in the early hours a passenger ferry, with hundreds of day trippers aboard, capsized and sank off the Belgian port of Zeebrugge...' I froze. Another disaster and what sounded like a high number of casualties. I got dressed and went out to buy the papers. The press carried reports of over a hundred casualties, with the situation changing hourly. For the vessel lay on its side in shallow water. 'Ferry sinks in 90 seconds!' screamed one headline. *Marques* had foundered in 45. Another headline sounded uncomfortably familiar: '...death swept in through the *Herald*'s open doors.'

Some days later, something extraordinary happened. Nicholas Ridley, the man who had played such a leading part in the *Marques* story, used this current disaster to make a bad-taste joke in the House of Commons. Referring to a colleague, currently steering a Bill through the House, he linked this to the recent tragedy to make a feeble attempt at a 'sick joke'. He stood up in the Chamber and said, 'He is the pilot of the bill but has not got his bow doors open...*ha ha ha!*'

For a few days, it was all anyone talked about. The Prime Minister was forced to demand that he issue an apology. I saw this as my chance and I wrote the following letter to the *Guardian*.

Sir,

As one who was bereaved in an earlier shipping disaster (my 18-year-old son Ben Bryant was lost aboard Marques, a British Sail Training vessel, just short of three years ago) I should like to make a personal comment on Nicholas Ridley's ill-judged reference to the recent ferry tragedy and also on the speed of this Government's reaction in this particular case. At the time of the Marques disaster, Nicholas Ridley was Transport Minister. His department was responsible for having issued the vessel with a load-line exemption certificate, having waived the statutory examination by DfT inspectors. After a year of no answers I wrote to Nicholas Ridley about this deviation from practice and urged him to call a public inquiry.

My letter to Mr Ridley was never answered but pressure, exerted elsewhere, resulted in a Public Inquiry being set up. Whilst I deplore this recent tragedy and applaud the government's prompt action in setting up an inquiry – and my heart goes out to the bereaved and injured – they can, in one sense, count themselves fortunate. The sheer scale of the tragedy was undoubtedly responsible for such prompt action being taken. It took a year and more for the Marques Inquiry to be announced and I say without fear of correction that without the pressure I was able to exert, there would have been no inquiry into this disaster in which 19 lost their lives. It is easy for Ministers and the PM to appear on television and present a caring image, where the high media profile and the scale of the tragedy, has made it politic for them to do so. One would be less cynical if the same prompt action applied in other tragedies, equally deserving of public concern, but which, for reasons of locale and scale, did not hit the media with quite the same force. This leads one to reflect whether the true face of government is not more truly revealed by Mr Nicholas Ridley than his more astute colleagues.

Yours

Shirley Cooklin

London, NW5

The second letter, on the same subject, was from a schoolteacher

Sir,

On Monday I discussed the Zeebrugge disaster with a class of second-formers at a comprehensive school in Dudley. The children had been appalled and upset at what they had seen. I

expanded their discussion to include the phenomenon of the 'sick joke' which invariably ensues after such a tragedy. I asked them to do a little research and let me know as soon as they heard such a joke. Little did I expect its first manifestation in the mass media rather than the playground and even less that its source should be a government minister

    Margaret Stilhard (Ms)

    Stourbridge

The icing on the cake was the third letter:

Sir,

Nicholas Ridley's comment was more than unfortunate. Just what barbarism lurks in his subconscious mind? So-called black humour may be used to question prejudices, or to relieve otherwise-intolerable situations, but neither apply here. This smack of an awful void where an everyday conscience should reside. In other circumstances this is commonly referred to as sociopathy. Is this man a sociopath, or does his life and his politics lead him to internalise sociopathic behaviour? If the former we should be profoundly worried that this person is in a position of control over others. If the latter then truly we are at the beginning of the end of any pretence of liberalism in this country.

No, Mrs Thatcher, an apology is profoundly inadequate.

    Yours

    Mike George

    London N8

A day or so later I received a letter from the *Guardian* Editor-in-Chief:

A FLY IN THE OINTMENT

Dear Shirley Cooklin,

Thanks for your interesting letter. I was glad to see, earlier, that your letter to the editor was given proper prominence. I thought the aftermath of the Marques tragedy was very bad. And you're right: it was one more victim of the collapse of serious opposition politics since 1979.

With good wishes,

Yours sincerely

Hugo Young

Meanwhile, the *Herald* continued to dominate the headlines. Then, ten days later, on 24 March, we re-assembled at Church House. After three years and 64 full days in court, we were faced with everything being overruled: this time, within the space of one day.

The new judgement began with these words: 'On the evidence of drawings and specifications – not available during the main part of the inquiry in 1985–86 – the barque was stable and seaworthy.'

I was in shock.

I whispered to Rupert, 'Surely they must bring Roger back?' But he shook his head. There was nothing to be said.

Outside on the steps afterwards, journalists crowded round. I stood blinking in the sunlight as Gareth Parry from the *Guardian* asked for my reaction. 'It will happen again,' I said. 'More people will die.'

Next day he wrote, 'Rupert Massey, representing the parents of Ben Bryant, told the final day of the formal investigation by the Wreck Commissioner in London: "...relatives of the dead man were filled with 'a sense of despair and foreboding'." Rupert was reported as saying, 'It is most curious that so much stability information has become available to the owner since the loss of this ship and the termination of this inquiry last June, when it was needed by the Department of Trade, yet none of it was available or thought necessary when considering using this trip for the training of young and inexperienced people.'

Facts and logistics were rehearsed and repeated and the column ended: 'Wreck Commissioner, Mr Richard Stone QC, closed the investigation saying that he anticipated producing his report in four to six weeks.'

32

A REPORT OUT OF *ALICE IN WONDERLAND*
LONDON, MARCH 1987

During the last weeks of March 1987, newspapers were flooded with stories of shipping disasters. It is sometimes said of London buses that they 'hunt in pairs', but you don't expect that of boats. Disaster at sea was almost becoming modish.

Time Out carried accounts of a rash of trawler deaths in the Irish Sea, with no fewer than 30 incidents of ships being 'snagged' by passing submarines, accompanied by a tragic loss of life. Another story was only too familiar: the Department for Transport was coming under pressure from a woman, whose brother, and four other crew, drowned when their boat sank in mysterious circumstances in February 1985. Another concerned the *Derbyshire*, a large merchant shipping vessel, whose long-delayed Public Inquiry was imminent. A report appeared in the *Guardian* about

The East Bridge, a sister-vessel, which had sailed for a scrap-yard in Taiwan, in spite of the fact that she was needed as evidence for a Public Inquiry. Both vessels were part of a fleet, built by the government-friendly Swan Hunter shipyard, and had the same structural defects. Jim Slater, President of the NUS (National Union of Seamen), claimed this would hinder collection of vital evidence which he needed for the Derbyshire Inquiry. He appealed to the DfT to send inspectors on board in Rotterdam and use their powers to prevent the ship from sailing (under Convention 147 of the International Labour Organization), but to no avail.

It seemed shipping disasters were everywhere. The Public Inquiry into the *Herald* disaster was due to begin on 27 April. A day or so later a letter arrived advising us that our report on *Marques* would be ready for collection at the DfT offices at Sunley House in the Strand. We were told to present ourselves at 1 p.m. precisely on 30 April. Peter came over and we drove through Camden Town, tense and silent. Going down Kingsway the traffic became deadlocked. We were moving inch by inch, with the lights always against us. As I rounded the corner into the Strand we heard the pips on the car radio and the announcer said *Marques* had been found unseaworthy. I clutched at Peter screaming, 'We've won!' He screamed back, 'For God's sake watch out, woman…you almost went into someone!' I parked outside Sunley House – double yellow lines everywhere. I was past caring, slammed on the brakes and tore into Sunley House with Peter in hot pursuit.

They were waiting for us at reception. There we were handed a thick brown A4 envelope that I tore open, then pulled out the thick document, to scan the first page and find the Summary, which was halfway down in bold:

...it was not the fault of any person or persons that Marques had insufficient stability to resist the said squall but if judged by the knowledge and experience now available the stability of Marques would be found to have been inadequate and the vessel unseaworthy for sail training in non-coastal waters.

Dated this 23rd day of April 1987. Signed R. H. Stone, Judge

After four years in court and more twists and turns than a hurricane, this was the court's conclusion: the boat had been unseaworthy, but it was no one's fault.

I turned to the clerk to ask if I could use her phone. I must speak to Nicola, who had produced the BBC *Newsnight* programme we had once believed would blow the whole story wide open. She picked up immediately. 'I've already heard it's a whitewash.'

The rest of that day was a blur. I can recall the first interview, which we gave in Rupert's Chambers, but not who it was for or what either of us said. After that, one venue seemed to merge into the next. We went by taxi, or what seemed like a magic carpet, from one interview to the next: from studio to office and street to studio, microphones and cameras everywhere. As dusk fell and the sky bled with the setting sun, it was time for the evening news, something we each of us wanted to hear at home. By now we were hoarse, speechless and could not have mustered another word.

For seven hours we had been interviewed, filmed, questioned all over London and must have said the same things, over and over again. For that day we were the news. Fuelled by anger and the memory of all that wasted effort. In the end, no matter whose fault, we had failed. It was a very long day: the longest I can ever remember.

33

THE END OF
THE *MARQUES* STORY

Press coverage rumbled on: people connected our story
with the *Herald* and the issue of 'safety at sea'.

On 17 May Victor Smart reported in the *Guardian* that
Counsel for DfT was blaming others, while Townsend
Thoresen and the National Union of Seamen said the
DfT should be in the dock, as '"procedures" were mani-
festly and inherently dangerous'.

In the months that followed, the press began calling
me 'Ben's Mum', a title I was happy to own. Letters
continued to flow to and from the US, with Roger, Bill
and Buzz. Bill had written to the Treasury Solicitor: '...
seaworthiness is the sufficiency of a vessel, for the service
in which it is employed': a rational statement. But
government are alchemists and can make things mean
what they wish. It was a lesson to me: politics is a very
dirty game.

Letters rained in. Hugo Young, *Guardian* Editor-in-Chief, had agreed that 'it was one more victim of the collapse of serious opposition politics' (he might have been talking about Brexit in 2019).

The report was published on 23 April. Afterwards, Rupert and I argued over what I should do next. He wanted me to become 'a litigant in person' but I did not want to become one of those people who spend their entire life pursuing a lost cause. I did agree, however, to issue a writ for damages against the government for Ben's death, which named Litchfield and Perryman and was widely reported in the press on 17 May.

On 20 May I had a letter from Karen Davidson, the US Attorney and my first contact in the USA. She wrote: '...I have received a copy of the report. I too think it a white-wash. It is appalling after such a thorough investigation that he was allowed to make such a ludicrous conclusion.' But it was not Mr Stone who was the culprit, it came from higher up in the food chain, from Ridley and Thatcher.

On 26 September we assembled in Stone's Chambers, for one last time. This was a 'costs' hearing, held in private, with no secretaries to take down our words. Dick Stone (as I was now allowed to call him) could express himself freely. To Belinda Bucknall, who had made an application for costs on behalf of Lloyd's of London, he said: 'The answer to your application is negative, Ms Bucknall. Of course I will not award you "costs". Your interest in this case was purely commercial.'

Then he turned to Litchfield and with something approaching venom, for such a mild man, said, 'Mr Litchfield, I do not know how you can have the effrontery to even ask. You cannot fail to be aware you are lucky to not be meeting the costs of the entire Inquiry.'

He granted costs to the Sail Training Association. Then he turned to me, saying that I had made a worthwhile contribution to the Inquiry and that costs would be granted in recognition.

When the hearing was over, I went outside to sit on one of the stone benches in the Inns of Court. Although I could not see him, I knew Ben or his soul was hovering. It was time to let him go. I knew he would be glad, that although I had not succeeded in what I set out to do, I had at least exposed the ugliness and the lies. Ben, throughout his short life, never told a lie and would have appreciated that. I craved one final conversation but knew that it was my need and not his. I remembered him saying, in that last-ever phone call, 'Don't worry, Mum, I'll keep in touch.' Ben would always be with me. The Rabbi had told me that Ben 'was an anarchist'. He had been his own man from the moment he was born. We had always given each other space and you cannot say fairer than that. I set him free and counted myself fortunate to have had his company for eighteen years.

EPILOGUE

34

A NEW NIGHTMARE
30 MAY 1995

The years rolled by until it was ten, then eleven, since the *Marques* disaster. One evening, towards the end of May 1995, I switched on the television to watch the news and saw an old sailing barque cross the screen. My heart almost stopped, as it looked like the ghost of *Marques*. But I knew only too well, whatever remained of her lay deep in the waters off Bermuda.

While I was still puzzling, the telephone shrilled. I picked up only to catch my breath, for the voice on the other end of the line was none other than Andrew Harvey. It was that same newscaster whom I had engaged with so often in the aftermath of the *Marques* disaster. But that was over a decade ago, so what was going on now? 'Good evening, it's the BBC. Might I speak to Shirley Cooklin?' Was this a dream or a nightmare? I heard myself say, 'Andrew, that vessel on the screen just now, was it...could it possibly be *Marques*?' I was startled to hear him reply, 'I was just about to ask you the same question.'

The lines were soon red hot, as calls crossed, and we tried to unravel the mystery. The vessel *looked* like *Marques*, but could not be her. For we knew, too well, that what remained of her, lay rotting on the ocean floor, in the waters off Bermuda. To add to the puzzle, we knew that her sister ship, the *Inca*, was in Canada. Having been impounded by lawyers and, so far as we knew, was rotting away in the Great Lakes, stuck in the mud and ravaged by powderpost beetle. The *Inca* had been the subject of lawsuits over the last ten years, by those who had lost loved ones on *Marques*. But that was eleven years ago. What was going on now?

We decided that somehow she had been resurrected – then spirited across the Atlantic. The mystery deepened as it became clear that it was indeed the *Inca*, sailing under a new name, the *Maria Assumpta*. The most alarming fact to emerge, was that she had just foundered off the coast of Cornwall. Even more astonishing was the fact that Mark Litchfield had been at the wheel. Three crew members were missing: a woman, a young man and a girl of the same age as Ben, when he died. Litchfield, we heard, had skipped to safety over the rocks. It was history repeating itself.

I felt sick. All that struggle for nothing. It had all happened again. I had stood outside that court eleven years ago, telling reporters, 'It will happen again.' Now it had. All those months, *years*, of battling for the truth: all for nothing. Now three more lives had been lost. But there was one difference this time: for Mark Litchfield himself had been at the wheel. What's more, yet again, he was blaming the wind. But the harbour-master was insisting he'd sailed too close to the shore and bluntly asserted the disaster was down to bad seamanship.

I offered to go in and make a statement but the BBC were wary. They had incurred heavy costs in the aftermath of the *Marques* disaster and got their fingers well and truly burnt. As it turned out, ITN stepped up and asked me to go in to appear live on the news. There I stood before a mic, blazing with anger, as ITN staff hung over balconies to watch. All I could see was Ben's angry young face. It had all happened again, as I had prophesied. As well as Mark Litchfield being at the wheel, there was something else: it had taken place off the British coast in Cornwall. Soon, British police were on the scene and there was talk of a charge of manslaughter.

After the first shock, the case disappeared for a while from the headlines. But Peter kept a sharp eye open for further news. In February 1996, he rang me to say that the case was finally going to trial. The charge, at Truro Crown Court, was manslaughter. Yet again, Litchfield's cronies came out in force, claiming it was just another case of *bad luck*. Then things went quiet again.

Months later, it emerged that British police had gone to Canada to chase the evidence. It was being said that the reason behind this second disaster was that the boat's engines had failed. Since they had been sourced from Canada, inquiries were going on there. Then we heard the shocking news that the engine failure had been due to the fact that the fuel had been adulterated with water. Had disaster really struck for the sake of a few coppers? After all, Mark Litchfield was a very rich man and had been on board himself. Then something else became clear: Litchfield's supporters were doing their best to get the case dropped. They even tried to nobble the Attorney General, Nicholas Lyell. But this misfired: Lyell saw red and redoubled his efforts. On 8 August 1997, at Truro Crown Court, Mark Litchfield was found guilty on a charge of manslaughter. Justice had finally caught up with him.

But it did not end there. With money no object this time, the case went to Appeal in the High Court. I was determined to be there when it was heard, hoping to see justice done. With two new cases of manslaughter – and a total tally of twenty-one deaths – it was surely time for Mark Litchfield to face justice.

35

THE ROYAL COURTS
OF JUSTICE
NOVEMBER 1997

After sixty-nine days in court that brought press hullaba-
loo, public concern and private pain, the day arrived. I got
stuck in traffic and so arrived late. The three scarlet-robed
High Court judges, in their full-bottomed wigs, were
already on the bench.

A man in a suit was standing before their Lordships,
giving evidence. I turned to the person next to me to ask
who he was. This individual wore a badge, telling the
world he was called Terry Eastwood and that he worked
for the Crown Prosecution Service. Assuming he would
know what was going on, I asked about the man in the
witness box. To my untutored eye, their Lordships seemed
to be giving him a very hard time.

'It's the CID officer who arrested Mark Litchfield.' We
watched as he was asked to hand over his notebook.

'Do they not believe him?'

'The Defence are claiming procedures were not followed.'

'He looks honest enough to me.'

When the questioning ended, the plain-clothes officer left the stand and the three High Court judges got into a huddle. I turned again to Terry Eastwood to ask what was happening now. He explained that the judges had decided they must confer among themselves. Due to that, the Court would now hold a recess. The judges retired and the rest of us got up to stretch our legs. I was standing next to the man who had been in the box. I murmured, 'They gave *you* a hard time. What was that all about?'

He looked startled, then said, 'I'm a policeman. That sort of thing goes with the territory. In my line of work, you have to learn to cultivate a thick hide.'

'Will he get off, do you think?'

'Not if I can help it.'

That cheered me up no end, so I began smiling. He gave me a rather odd look and said, 'What's your interest in the case?'

'It's not the case I'm interested in – it's the man. He killed my son.'

'I'm sorry to hear that. When was this?'

'Eleven years ago.'

'Was it a road accident?'

'No, at sea. And by the way, it was no accident.'

I told my new friend the story of the *Marques* tragedy.

311

'What a dreadful tale. My condolences. But bravo for making a stand. I cannot imagine losing a child.'

'That's why I'm here. I want to see justice done.'

'Nothing will bring your son back.'

'No, but I said that that man would do it again. He has killed enough people. It must stop. We fought hard for almost three years. But he was Siamese twins with a government minister and got clean off the hook. But *this time* there is no one else to carry the can.'

'And you took this on as a private citizen?'

'I was forced to. I could not let my son down. He would have expected me to stand up for him. I had no choice. Someone must stand up for the dead.'

He looked at me curiously. 'May I ask your name?'

'It's Shirley,' I said. 'But why do you ask?'

'It's not every day you come across someone who will take on a government. You stood up for your son and I salute you for that.'

'Don't forget the other eighteen.'

'Nineteen people were killed at a stroke?'

'Yes. May I ask *your* name?'

'Alex. That cannot have been easy.' He shook his head, 'Fancy joining me for a cup of tea?'

'Is there a restaurant here?'

'It's more a canteen and it's down in the bowels of the old crypt.'

'Lead on,' I said.

Down we went and, as our conversation continued, I warmed to this individual who seemed to understand my compulsion for justice.

'You are clearly a feisty lady...' he said, smiling. '...I must take care to not get on your wrong side.'

'Now you're laughing at me.'

'Not at all. I have a daughter myself and cannot begin to imagine losing her.'

'What's your view, will he get off this charge?'

'Not if I have anything to do with it.'

Something was puzzling me, and, as here was the horse's mouth, I asked him a question. 'In this latest case he was *on board* as skipper. Yet it seems that he used adulterated fuel to save a few coppers. The man is a millionaire. That seems strange to me.'

'Yes, he has me baffled.'

'The vessel on which my son died sank because he'd skimped on repairs. But this time he was risking his *own* life.'

Alex said, 'My impression of Mr Litchfield is that he is someone who thinks the rules don't apply to him. He is an arrogant man.'

'You are right there, Alex.'

Suddenly he rose, his face pale. 'I've just noticed my colleague has gone back. They must have begun.'

The next moment we were heading fast for the lift.

Alex was right on the money, for we were late. By the time we reached the courtroom, the three High Court judges had already pronounced their verdict. All those years waiting for justice and I had missed the big moment. I was standing next to Terry Eastwood once again and grabbed at his sleeve to hiss, 'What's happening?' He gave me a rather strange look and replied, 'As you can see, the Appeal has failed and Mr Litchfield is now on his way down to the cells to begin his sentence.' I turned and saw that he was right. But I had prepared myself for failure, so asked anxiously, 'Are you *sure?*'

Quite suddenly, Ben manifested, like the genie in Ali Baba.

'Oh, Mum...' he cried, '...you really are *the end.*'

And finally, it was...

THE END

ACKNOWLEDGEMENTS

First, to my editor Ajda Vucicevic, for the inspirational way she brought this story to print. It was a long journey but we got there in the end.

Ian Levine and David Brawn, who set the ball rolling.

The friends who had faith, both in me and the book. Could not have done it without you, Mary-Ann and Emma.

My agent Jane Graham Maw, for her wisdom, patience and guidance.

Thank you to Daisy Ward for practically everything.

Justin Marozzi and Rory MacLean, who began it at Avon.

And to all who sail – may you always come ashore safely.